THE JOSEPH WILLIAMS S… …USIC
UNDER THE EDITORSHI… …MACPHERSON.

MUSIC
AND ITS APPRECIATION
OR
THE FOUNDATIONS OF TRUE LISTENING

NEW AND REVISED EDITION

BY

STEWART MACPHERSON

AUTHOR OF
"*Form in Music*," "*Practical Harmony*,"
"*Melody and Harmony*,"
ETC.

Price 6/– net

LONDON:
JOSEPH WILLIAMS, LIMITED
29 ENFORD STREET, MARYLEBONE, W.1
U.S.A. - THE B. F. WOOD MUSIC CO., BOSTON

B 190 [MADE AND PRINTED IN GREAT BRITAIN]

TABLE OF CONTENTS.

BATH
SPA
UNIVERSITY
Library

B.S.U.C. - LIBRARY
00343997

TO THE LATE

PROFESSOR FREDERICK NIECKS.

FOREWORD.

"See deep enough, and you see musically."—CARLYLE.

THE present volume is primarily intended for the amateur; it is an attempt to shew the music-lover how much is lost to him if he is content to regard music as a more or less agreeable sensation, *et praeterea nihil.* It says little, probably, which the professional student of music has not heard many times before—or with which he has not come into contact in some way or another during the period of his studentship.

The author has, however, often felt that there is a vast mass of real musical intelligence existing outside the ranks of specialized music-students which only needs a stimulus in the right direction for it to become a most valuable and powerful factor in the musical life of the community. The art of music above all things needs more cultivated and discriminating listeners, listeners who *really hear what the composer has written.* Curious as it may seem, this power is far less universal than may possibly be imagined; indeed it may without exaggeration be said that it is only a minority who possess it in any marked degree. Many hear only "the tune," and have no realization of the bass, or of the inner parts of the harmony; they hear *something* supporting that tune, perhaps; but it is confused and indistinct, and presents no form or shape to their mind and sense. To others the ability to perceive detail is utterly wanting, and as a consequence many a moment of exquisite delight is entirely lost to them.

It is true that, after all, one must take in a work of art as a whole—as a synthesis of its various parts and details; but a point that too often is overlooked in the case of music is that, if we can train our children from their early days to observe with their ears, as well as with their eyes, the apprehending of detail—at first a conscious act, like everything else of the kind—

becomes as time goes on an act that is subconscious and almost effortless. Such matters as we have been referring to then fit into the general scheme of things, and take their proper place in the true appreciation of the composer's work.

The subject of vocal and dramatic music, though of the highest interest, clearly could not be treated of adequately in the space available in the present volume, which deals therefore almost exclusively with the question of instrumental music—its material and form, and the characteristic features of the various periods in its history.

In a certain sense, music unallied to poetry or the drama, depending entirely upon its own beauty of outline and its inherent power of expression, makes demands of a special nature upon the perception of the listener, and it is in this direction, perhaps, more than in any other, that the average hearer needs guidance in his listening. In the hope of supplying in some measure this need, the following pages have been written. That they cover all the ground that is to be covered, the author does not for a moment pretend; but if they in any way have the effect of inciting the general music-lover to a deeper study of the meaning and intention of the masters who have written for our delight, he will feel that, however inadequate his treatment of his subject may have been, his efforts will not entirely have failed in the purpose to which they have been dedicated.

LONDON, 1940.

INDEX TO MUSICAL EXAMPLES.

The Author is indebted to the following firms for kind permission to print extracts from their publications:—

Messrs. Bote & Bock, Berlin, for those marked ... *
" Fromont, Paris, for those marked ... †
" Jurgenson, Moscow, for those marked... ‡
" Lengnick & Co., " " ... §
" Peters, Leipzig, " " ... ‖
" Schott & Co., " " ... **

*** The numbering of the Symphonies and Pianoforte Sonatas of Haydn and Mozart throughout this volume is that of Peters' edition.

*** The various instruments mentioned in Chapter XII. are obtainable from Messrs. Hawkes & Son, who have courteously supplied the illustrations. Thanks are also due to Messrs. Boosey & Co. for permission to reproduce the illustration of the Cor Anglais.

MUSIC AND ITS APPRECIATION

OR

THE FOUNDATIONS OF TRUE LISTENING.

CHAPTER I.

INTRODUCTORY.

It is hardly too much to say that one of the penalties the Anglo-Saxon race pays for its vaunted and undoubted common-sense and hard-headedness is that, speaking generally, it has rarely been inclined to take art seriously, or to regard it in the light of anything more than a harmless amusement. Until quite recently, the idea of spending a certain amount of time and trouble in order to appreciate a noble picture or a musical work of lofty aim would hardly have occurred to the average man as a necessary preliminary to the summing-up of its merits or demerits, or even to the possibility of a true enjoyment of its contents. Of all the arts, music has suffered from this attitude the most; people who will hesitate before giving their opinion upon a great poem or even a great picture seem to have no such becoming modesty in the presence of the Divine Art, but, "rushing in where angels fear to tread," will, in the airiest manner, pass judgment upon the work of the musician without for a moment considering whether they possess the requisite qualifications for doing so, or not.

Preliminary training in order to appreciate truly.

But it should surely be recognized that the arriving at a standard of true judgment must mean that something in the nature of a preliminary training shall be undergone by those who wish to possess it, and it is at least a hopeful sign that this fact is gradually being perceived by many of those responsible for the more educative treatment of the art of music amongst the young.

In all really great work, be it literary, pictorial, musical, or what not, there is undoubtedly an *elemental something* which appeals to most of us with a sense of truth; but this does not necessarily indicate that we grasp its meaning, or appreciate its art. This must be the result of conscious effort; if we would really appreciate to the full, we must use our own faculties to the full. With regard to music, it has been well said, "It is not enough to place ourselves in a room where music is going on; we must by concentrated attention absorb and mentally digest it. Without the help of the alert mind, the ear can no more hear than the eye can see. . . . To approach sounds in such a way as to make sense of them—that is the art of listening to music."*

Conscious effort in appreciating.

In the case of the many who throng our concert-rooms, we shall not be very wide of the mark in saying that music reaches them purely as a physical sensation. A kind of "general impression" is produced, which presumably affords them a certain degree of pleasure; but it is quite incontestible that, in the majority of cases, the pure, unalloyed delight in the composer's art, arising from an appreciation of the actual language he uses, and of the development and interplay of his ideas, is something outside the experience of such hearers.

General Impression v. appreciation of beauty of detail.

Fondness for music—or, rather, the mere sensation of pleasure in hearing it—is not, however, of necessity a proof of sound judgment or appreciation, or indeed of the possession of the faculties requisite for true listening. The intelligent apprehending of music requires much that goes far beyond this; it requires the healthy development of the hearing sense—that sense which too often is left untrained and undeveloped in early life, partly for the reason that the bulk of the community regard the act of listening to music as something so obvious and familiar that any idea of preparation for such listening comes home to them with a feeling of strangeness and of novelty.

Development of the hearing sense.

It is true that certain kinds of music produce with tolerable ease an effect on the nerves which may easily be mistaken by those who experience it for the truer response of the musical faculties to which reference has just been made. It is not, however, by any means an infallible proof of a really musical organization, or of a power of apprehending music, that we should find such a piece as the "Ride of the Valkyries," or Tschaïkowski's "1812" overture setting up a certain kind of excitement in our nervous system, or that we should find ourselves instinctively beating time to the easily-

Effect of certain music on the nervous system.

* Surette & Mason—"The Appreciation of Music."

recognized rhythm of some (perhaps perfectly artistic) dance-measure. Of course, some whose knowledge of music as an art is very slight, and whose ears are in no way able to appreciate the countless beautiful details of a great work, are yet able to feel in a more or less vague manner the general emotional purport of such a work. Such persons are usually musical by nature, and should, it is clear, make the best listeners; but it is too often the case that they rest content with this ability merely to receive broad impressions, and are even wont to declare that, if they were to use their mental powers more, they would be in danger of losing the "soul" of the music! This curious glorification of ignorance is, to say the least, passing strange to those who know the joy that comes from that alert use of the mind and of the hearing sense which reveals so much of beauty and of interest which otherwise would be entirely lost.

Mere emotional appreciation.

The alert ear.

Finally, it may be urged that music is meant in the first place to be a refreshment and a solace, something which needs less an active, than a passive frame of mind. Without doubt music can in a very special way come to us with a touch that is at once restful and recreating; but it should be none the less borne in mind that refreshment and solace need not be synonymous with mental idleness, nor rest with *inertia* and a "vacuum of the brain." Of one thing we may be certain; that although each step forward in the art of listening may cost some effort, it will invariably bring with it some new delight, some new point of view unrealized before, which will be proof—if proof were needed—that the effort is worth the making.

CHAPTER II.

THE REQUISITES FOR TRUE LISTENING.

In the foregoing chapter it was stated that one of the essential conditions of true listening was that of real, earnest attention.

The composer, we may be sure, wishes us to hear what he has to tell us, not in a sleepy, unintelligent way, but in such a spirit of alertness that the countless beautiful points over which he has taken so much care shall enter our minds with that sense of interest and of delight which he intends they shall produce. Ruskin somewhere lays down the statement that the real appreciation of any art must include the apprehending of its details; judged by this standard, it is not too much to say that the kind of listening many persons think good enough for the art of the musician falls lamentably short of what it should, and might, be!

Average listening falls short of what it should be.

When we are called upon to listen to music, particularly instrumental music, what is there, then, to which our thoughts must be directed, if we would approach it in a spirit of true understanding? There are, clearly, many things to which it is necessary that some consideration must be given, and it will be convenient to set these out in order as a series of questions which the would-be listener may ask himself at such times:—

Points necessary in true listening.

(i) What is the nature of the composition—that is, is it Sonata, Symphony, Quartet, Romance, Impromptu, Fugue, or what?

(ii) For what instruments is it written? Is it for a complete orchestra, or for stringed-instruments, or, perhaps, the Piano alone?

(iii) What is its approximate date?

(iv) What are its chief themes or melodies? Can one seize upon these and remember them in such a way that their subsequent development may be clear to one's mind, and therefore a source of real interest?

(v) *How* does the composer so develop his ideas?

(vi) What is the Form of the work? Can one follow to any extent the composer's plan?

(vii) Can one in any sense follow and appreciate the subtle effects of harmony (*i.e.*, the chords) with which the composer supports and enriches his themes or melodies?

Let us briefly consider each of these points:—

(i) *What is the nature of the composition?*

Of course, some clue is usually afforded by the mere title of the work. For instance, if it is entitled a Valse or a Funeral March we shall know within certain limits what to expect as to its general trend and purport; if it is described as a Pianoforte Sonata, we shall not look for the assistance of a full orchestra, and so forth. But, beyond such very clear and elementary distinctions, the ideas of many persons as to the very nature of the compositions to which they listen are extraordinarily vague. It is not too much to say that there are very many amongst those who consider themselves rather musical, who would be hard put to it to describe the difference, for example,

The nature and character of what we may be called upon to hear.

between a Sonata and a Symphony, an Overture and a Concerto, a Cantata and an Oratorio!

Here, then, at the very outset, some little knowledge is requisite if we would find ourselves in condition for apprehending any work we may be called upon to hear.

(ii) *For what instrument, or instruments, is it written?*

Need for some power of distinguishing qualities of tone.

Here again, in order that we may appreciate to any satisfactory extent the wonderful effects of instrumental colouring which composers know so well nowadays how to employ, and which enter so largely into their scheme, it is of real importance that we should be able, with some degree of certainty, to recognize the peculiar qualities of the various instruments which they use—to distinguish, for example, between a Violin and a Viola, a Violoncello and a Double-Bass (not merely by their appearance, but by their sound); to listen to a passage played, say, by an Oboe in the orchestra, and not to confuse it with one played by a Clarinet, and so on. If this is impossible, much of what we hear reaches us imperfectly, and our appreciation will be correspondingly imperfect, our power of true enjoyment hampered and hindered beyond belief.

(iii) *What is its approximate date?*

Importance of realizing the period at which a composition was written.

It is probable that such a question as this is generally the last that ever occurs to the majority of persons to ask themselves when face to face with a work of art, particularly of musical art. And yet in music, perhaps more than in anything else, the approximate date is all-important as affording a practically infallible clue to its style and character. For a continuous development of the most interesting kind has been going on, of the highest significance in the progress of the art; men have, as it were, "built upon one another's shoulders" in a very special and notable way, and the work of one generation has been rendered possible simply by reason of the achievements of the previous generation. This has been the case with music much more markedly than with literature or the other arts. Poetry, painting and sculpture have in all ages been based upon ideas and facts outside themselves; they have been men's endeavours, in different ways, to illustrate or represent certain definite objects or ideas, and consequently—even from their earliest days—there has always been something with which they could be compared, to test their truthfulness and their worth.

Music, on the other hand, has had no such help from outside; it has in all ages come from within, simply as an expression of something in the artist's own consciousness. The result of this is that the growth of music has, until the last three or four centuries, been laboriously slow. When the arts of architecture and sculpture were at their zenith, over two thousand years ago in Greece, music was just lisping in a kind of backward infancy. These last three or four hundred years though, have witnessed the most amazing advance, an advance quite unequalled in rapidity and power in the whole range of the history of intellectual achievement—at any rate, upon the literary or artistic side. The Venus of Milo and the Parthenon at Athens are still the despair of our sculptors and architects; but no one would, even for a moment, fall into the error of regarding the following passage as the despair of the modern musician!

Late growth of the musical art.

CONRAD PAUMANN.—Organ Piece (15th Century).

When we compare such a piece as this, so elementary in design and expression, with the marvellous power and beauty, the perfect technical mastery of a sonata of Bethoven or a music-drama of Wagner, it will be evident how far music has travelled in a little over four hundred years.

These are, of course, two extremes, and their difference is apparent to the dullest comprehension; but the value to the listener of some historical knowledge and perception lies in gaining the power of following the "romance and adventure" of the development of the musical art by being able, with experience, to recognize periods—at any rate, to some extent—by the character of the music. In this way, he will not expect to find in Mozart the kind of musical ideas he is accustomed to associate with Wagner, or to anticipate the peculiar sentiment of a Tschaïkowski in the works of Bach! He will thus be saved from the very common but disastrous error of forcing such things into a comparison as unjust as it is ignorant and foolish.

Unjust comparisons.

(iv) *Can we seize upon and remember the chief themes or melodies of the work to which we are listening?*

This is vitally necessary, if we are in any way to follow the uses to which the composer puts the ideas that come to him as an inspiration. For it is just by this *use* of his ideas that he brings his work into the realm of art. It is one thing to invent a more or less beautiful tune (very often a shepherd on a hill-side has done that); it is quite another thing to know what to do with it when it has to form part of the scheme of an elaborate composition. Such a tune is, so to speak, no more than the raw material out of which the composer must construct his work, and he can shew himself an artist only in so far as he can expand, develop, and bring out the possibilities of this material in a consistent and effective way.

Ideas and their uses.

The composer's "idea" his raw material.

It will often be found that the themes which transfix our attention in listening are those whose "essence," as it were, is concentrated in some terse, pithy idea of just a few notes, out of which much, if not the whole, of a composition frequently seems to germinate, like some plant or tree from a tiny seedling.

Striking themes.

Thus it is that Beethoven, with that splendid mastery of resource that distinguishes his writing, so often causes entire movements to spring into being from one or two "germ-ideas," which, like the initial theme of the C minor symphony—

BEETHOVEN.—Symphony No. 5, in C minor.

are as to size relatively unimportant, and even insignificant; but—as the sequel proves—are fruitful in possibilities of development of the most remarkable order.

(v) *How does the composer so develop his ideas?*

Every instrumental work of importance has of necessity some central thought upon which our attention must be focussed, just as a picture has its central figure or figures, a poem its dominant idea, a novel or a play its principal character or characters. In a picture the chief outstanding

The central thought in a musical work.

figure will in all probability be brought prominently into the foreground, and our minds thus impressed with its significance; in music, the composer's central idea will derive its importance largely through *repetition*—not bald re-statement, but judicious repetition under varied treatment, by which means whatever striking qualities it may possess in itself will be enhanced and emphasized.

The element of Repetition in music.

Thematic development.

An admirable illustration of this process of "thematic development," as it is often conveniently called, is afforded by the principal theme of the first movement of Beethoven's Symphony No. 1, in C, which opens thus:—

BEETHOVEN.—Symphony No. 1, in C.

This theme, as its after treatment shows, resolves itself into three separate and very notable figures, indicated above by the letters (*a*), (*b*) and (*c*). In the course of his work, Beethoven discusses each of these, and their development is full of interest and life. The following extracts will give us some little idea of his method of procedure:—

The above passages are conclusive evidence of the importance of the *figure*, or "germ-idea," in the composer's scheme.

The composer's "germ-idea."

In its original form a comparatively easily recognized group of notes, with a distinct rhythmic shape and character, such a figure germinates and expands in countless ways, our interest thus being continually stimulated. On the other hand, our sense of unity and consistency of purpose on the part of the composer is none the less surely satisfied by our realization of the fact that, amidst all the changes of character and feeling that are brought about by his treatment of the theme, it is *still that same theme* which is the "seed" from which so much has sprung into blossom.*

It is necessary here again to insist upon the fact that mere literal and bald repetition does not constitute the development of an idea. "There is just the contrast between the two that there is between a poor speaker, who keeps repeating the same word or phrase with futile emphasis, and the man of real eloquence, who follows a train of thought no less closely, but manages constantly to cast his ideas in new phraseology and fresh figures of speech, so that the variety of what he says is quite as striking as its fundamental unity."†

Distinction between bald repetition and true development.

(vi) *What is the Form of the work? Can one to any extent follow the composer's plan?*

It is a somewhat curious fact that, to many persons, the idea that a piece of music has a "form" comes with a sense of strangeness and of novelty. They fondly think that all that a composer has to do is to sit at his desk, pen in hand, and that, somehow, not only will ideas immediately be forthcoming, but the whole work, complete in all its details, will come into being—Minerva-like—without any sort of effort of will or concentration of brain-power on the writer's part! This, unfortunately, is a popular view of "inspiration," as ludicrous—if one thinks about the matter even for a moment—as it is false and pernicious. It gives no credit to the composer for the possession of **brains**, or for the use of them, but regards him merely as the passive recipient of thoughts over which he himself exercises little or no control. It is true that no mere cleverness will of itself produce a Shakespeare drama, a Rafaelle Madonna, a Beethoven symphony; the idea, *in embryo*, comes from a Higher Power; but the working-out of that idea, the bringing it to perfection, is the result of intelligence, of hard study, and of technical acquirements of a high order. Such matters as symmetry and balance of design, contrasts of colour, perspective, periods of repose and of climax, have to be considered, and the composer has to *shape* his work in such a way that we shall be sensible, not only of his power of emotional expression, but of his mastery of the "architecture" of the music—a mastery which tells us unmistakably that the "form" of his production is good.

Popular fallacies as to a composer's methods of work.

Inspiration—what it is, and what it is not.

---

* Other aspects of repetition in music will be touched upon later in connexion with Rhythm and Form (Chapter III).

† Surette & Mason—"The Appreciation of Music."

Of the various manifestations of Form in music there will be many occasions to speak later in this volume; it must suffice here to say that, broadly considered, it signifies the presentation of musical ideas in such a way that, when they are placed in connexion with, or relation to, one another, they may produce an intelligible and consistent result.

Form.

(vii) *Can one in any sense follow and appreciate the subtle effects of Harmony (i.e., the chords) with which the composer supports and enriches his melodies?*

It may, without fear of contradiction, be said that to the majority of people the first essential of enjoyment is the presence of melody, or tune. Tune is, in some ways, the most easily apprehended factor in music; and, provided that it is fairly strong in rhythm, and is kept above its accompaniment, thus :—

Tune.

is, usually, soon grasped by those who have any perception of musical sounds at all.

And, of course, it need hardly be said that there is nothing to be ashamed of in being fond of a good tune; but, at the same time, it is important to remember that, however expressive such a tune may be, the delight experienced by many in listening to it does not in any very special way denote the possession of a high degree of real musical appreciation. That depends on something beyond the mere pleasure in the regular periods of a mere tune, however beautiful. It is no more than a truism to say that many a popular melody which, with its piquant, rhythmic lilt and ear-catching outline, seizes us at a first hearing, so palls upon us with increased familiarity with its shallow prettiness, that not only does the zest with which we greeted it at first begin rapidly to die down, but whatever vestige of attractiveness it seemed ever to possess disappears altogether, and we heartily wish we had never heard it at all,—and, indeed, would go miles to get out of its way! Between such ephemeral compositions and the art of the true musician there is an utter difference, not only of degree, but of kind. In the tune from the comic opera or

The "catchy" tune.

from that insane product of our times, the musical play, the one thing that is obvious is its strongly-marked rhythm, with its regularly recurring pattern—that rhythm which soon wearies because it *is* so obvious. The harmony by which it is accompanied and supported is usually of the most elementary and flimsy description consisting as it often does of a threadbare, stereotyped formula, which crops up merrily in almost every composition of this kind:—

Poverty-stricken harmony.

It may be said with truth that in nothing is the art of the musician more clearly shewn than in the interest and expressiveness of his harmony; in nothing is the work of the true composer so surely distinguished from that of the mere "jingler." His harmony, be it observed, need not of necessity be elaborate, complicated, or abstruse—though, on the other hand, it may for some special purpose exhibit all these attributes—but it will exemplify the rare element of fitness, of inevitableness, by which we experience that sense of sincerity and truth of expression which is the "sign manual" of the artist, as distinct from the mere artizan.

The interest of the true composer's harmony.

Its inevitableness.

Thus we come face to face with a fact of the greatest importance—one which it is most necessary to observe—namely, that so intimately are melody and harmony bound up with one another in the composer's conception that they are in reality inseparable and mutually dependent.

One or two examples will make this clear. If we were to play the following strain of melody on the pianoforte, it is hardly too much to say that, to anyone who did not know the extract, and who consequently would be unable mentally to supply the harmonic colouring, it would appear a very ordinary and even commonplace succession of notes:—

Melody and harmony really inseparable.

When, however, the passage is invested with the harmonies imagined by its composer as a necessary condition of its very existence, the noble dignity of the 2nd subject of Beethoven's "Waldstein" sonata stands revealed :—

Again, to illustrate how the very life-breath of a melody depends—contrary often to popular ideas on the subject—upon its harmonic clothing, it is only necessary to accompany some beautiful and shapely tune with harmonies inappropriate to it, for us to discover at once that all its expressiveness—indeed, all its meaning—has been destroyed.

Let the dreamy poetry, the yearning, the "pliability" of the opening of Wagner's "Preislied" be noted :—

Bad harmony.

and then compared with the utterly sterile, unyielding, meaningless travesty presented by the following :—

and it will not be long before even the most average musical intelligence will be able to realize with some degree of clearness how much of the very beauty usually associated entirely with the melody, is in actual fact derived from the appropriateness and living interest of the harmony.*

Progress of music remarkable in the growth of harmony.

In nothing, save in the art of orchestral effect, has the progress of music been more strongly marked than in the increasing interest, power and expressiveness of its harmony, and it stands to reason that, when a composer seeks to make his music reflect the deeper emotions, it is likely that his harmony—and even his melody—will be less obvious, less easily grasped fully on a first hearing. Thus it comes about that, to the careless or unthinking hearer, such music—coupled with the absence of an ear-catching rhythm—makes, and will make, little or no appeal, simply for the reason that he is not putting himself in the right condition for listening.

Therefore, to conclude this rapid survey of the chief requisites for true listening, it must again be insisted upon that such true listening entails a certain amount of trouble ; nothing less than whole-hearted, intelligent attention is necessary for the matter, if we would enter into the thoughts of the composer, and follow what he has to tell us in a spirit of real appreciation.

---

* Comparing the art of the musician with that of the painter, it might be said that melody corresponds, roughly speaking, to line-drawing—to pleasant curves and shapely outlines ; harmony to those lights and shadows which, more than all else, impart the touch of emotion and of humanity to the picture.

CHAPTER III.

THE SIMPLER ASPECTS OF MUSICAL CONSTRUCTION—RHYTHMIC SHAPE.

If we take any simple piece, such as one of the National tunes in which these Islands of ours are so rich, we shall find that the sense of satisfaction such a tune produces in our minds results, not merely from the rise or fall of the notes themselves, but from something else which in a very special sense renders these notes—the melody, that is—intelligible.

In other words, we shall find that there are certain points in its course which stand out as "landmarks," as it were. To each of these landmarks all that goes before seems to tend; they are in a sense points of repose: they "punctuate" the music, and help to give it that feeling of shapeliness which the ear almost instinctively demands.

The "punctuation" of music.

This desire for a certain orderliness in the setting forth of a composer's ideas has resulted in what is known as Rhythm or Rhythmic shape. This term, unfortunately, has been given many meanings and has been used with many different applications; frequently it is confused with Time, and one often hears such expressions as $\frac{3}{4}$ Rhythm, Quadruple Rhythm, and so on; or, as likely as not, it is regarded as signifying the same as Accentuation. Thus, the following passages, although identical in Time, would often be said to be different in Rhythm:—

Rhythm.

But it seems on all grounds clearer and more useful to confine our use of the word Rhythm to the division of the music into more or less clearly defined periods which—like the grouping of words into sentences—makes what we hear or read clear to our mind. Music is so "punctuated" in its course by its rising or falling to definite points called *Cadences*, which correspond to the stops used in writing a

Explanation of the term.

Cadences and their effect.

language. These Cadences may be grouped under three headings, according as they give the impression of—

(i) Conclusion, or rest.

(ii) Incompletion—a mere temporary break in the course of the music.

(iii) Interruption or surprise.

Here is a familiar instance of the first of these varieties of musical punctuation:—

Naturally the most obvious position for a Cadence producing such a feeling of conclusion is at the end of a composition, or of an important division of it; therefore, as a general rule, composers reserve the *Perfect Cadence* (as it is called), in its most emphatic shape, for such points in their writing.*

The Perfect Cadence.

To continue our analogy with literature, therefore, we may say that the Perfect Cadence corresponds roughly to the full-stop occurring at the end of a sentence or paragraph, where the sense, for the time being, is more or less complete.

It is easy to see, though, that the too frequent use of such a strongly-marked point of repose would tend to cut up the music into a series of small sections which would entirely destroy all idea of continuity. Consequently we find the various periods in its course punctuated in such a way as to allow of the listener's attention and interest being carried forward from moment to moment. This is achieved by the use of those less decisive Cadences which produce in the mind the effect either of (i) temporary rest, but uncompleted sense; or (ii) surprise or interruption.

Continuity in music.

The Half-Cadence.

The first of these effects is usually supplied by the *Imperfect* or *Half-Cadence*:—†

---

* The Perfect Cadence is sometimes used as a "middle" Cadence, when its strong conclusive effect is modified in some way, usually by the avoidance of the key-note in the melody of the final chord.

† The many varieties of this form of Cadence cannot, in the nature of things, be given here; it must suffice to say that these are practically endless. The example quoted furnishes a very usual instance.

"The Banks of Allan Water."

&c.

In this instance the impression created is very much the same as that of a comma or a semi-colon in writing; we are conscious that the music gains in clearness by the slight break or division, but that we nevertheless are impelled to listen attentively for what is going to follow, if we would gather any idea of the true and complete meaning of the passage.

The Interrupted Cadence.

The second effect mentioned above—that of surprise or interruption—is generally associated with the *Interrupted Cadence.* The judicious use of such a form of Cadence is of the highest value to a composer, for it is particularly true in the art of music that "the unexpected is always happening." By this we do not mean that the listener is subjected to a series of mental shocks, but that his interest continually receives fresh impetus through some new and unanticipated—but none the less welcome—"turn of events," either in the melody or the harmony. In good music such happenings as these produce the greater delight from their inevitableness—from our sense, that is, that the composer after all could not have said what he had to say in a more effective and convincing way. How true this is will, we think, be readily perceived by a perusal of the following passages. The first contains two Interrupted Cadences (at (*a*) and (*b*)), causing a two-fold postponement of the Perfect Cadence, which is all the more welcome when it eventually appears:—

Adagio. MOZART.—Fantasia in C minor.

Our second example, from the last act of "Die Meistersinger," shews us a most delightful interruption of the expected Perfect Cadence by the chord at (*c*), by which the music is diverted, so to speak, into another channel and a complete change of thought brought about. In the Opera, Walther von Stolzing, the hero of the drama, has just finished his well-known "Prize-Song," and the following extract is taken from the chorus in which—to the music of the song—the people acclaim him victor. The interruption at (*c*) to which we have just alluded as marking a change of feeling, is the point at which the cobbler-poet, Hans Sachs, steps forward and asks the assembled crowd whether he was not justified in his admiration for the song and in his belief in its author:—

Moderato molto. WAGNER.—"Die Meistersinger."

In much simple music, cadences occur with a greater or less degree of regularity and divide it into easily-recognized periods, mostly of four bars in length, termed *Phrases*. Such a phrase is to be seen in the example on page 17. It is clear, however, that this particular phrase cannot stand by itself, as the cadence at its termination is such as to create a desire in the mind for something more to follow. This is almost always the effect of a *single phrase*, which needs at least one other phrase of somewhat similar character to act as a sort of natural response to it, and to impart that feeling of balance which the ear desires. Let us see how the writer of the song, "On the Banks of Allan Water," meets this requirement:—

Musical Phrases.

Need for a responsive phrase.

If the above extract be played it will be noticed that the two phrases balance one another in a manner not unlike that of the rhyming of the lines in a stanza of poetry, *e.g.*:—

Rhyming in music.

O had we some bright little isle of our own,
In a blue summer ocean far off and alone.

Another example of the response of phrase to phrase in this way is shewn in the following delightful Old English tune:—

"Barbara Allen."

In dance-music, in order to correspond to, and fit in with, the movements of the dancers, these four-bar phrases occur one after another in a regular succession; in many national tunes and folk-songs, too, this consistent "rhyming" is noticeable in large measure, for the reason that the music closely follows the accent and metre of the words to which it is set. And, even in music not connected with dancing or with poetic stanzas, such regularity of rhythm frequently prevails throughout the greater part of a composition, especially where that composition keeps within a limited range as to length.*

Regularity of phrases.

When, however, a composer is writing upon a larger scale, or when he wishes to produce the idea of stress and passion, such squareness of phrase is no longer always in place. Then it is that the rhythm from time to time becomes more complicated; the music often ceases to come to points of repose at the expected places, it is more continuous, and flows on for some considerable time without any apparent break, producing an impression of intensity by the avoidance of those very "breathing places" which, in the ordinary course of things, are not only desirable, but necessary. It thus gathers force and impetus as it proceeds, until it reaches its culmination at a point of climax or of rest, whose effect is enhanced by the manner in which the composer has led up to it. An

More complicated and continuous rhythms.

Working to a climax.

* See such pieces as Chopin's Mazurkas, Schumann's "Album for the Young," many of Grieg's "Lyrische Stückchen," &c.

extract from the overture to Wagner's "Meistersinger" will provide us with an admirable illustration of such a proceeding:—

The magnificent "uplift" of the whole of this fine passage is largely due to the absence of frequent rhythmic divisions of a strongly-marked character; the music is not rhythm*less*, but the periods are rendered less obvious by various means, amongst which that particular kind of repetition in music we have described in Chapter II (page 8) as *Thematic development* holds an important place. This is particularly observable in bars 5–13 and 16–18, where the sense of gathering strength is intimately bound up with the expansion of the two "figures"—

Important figures.

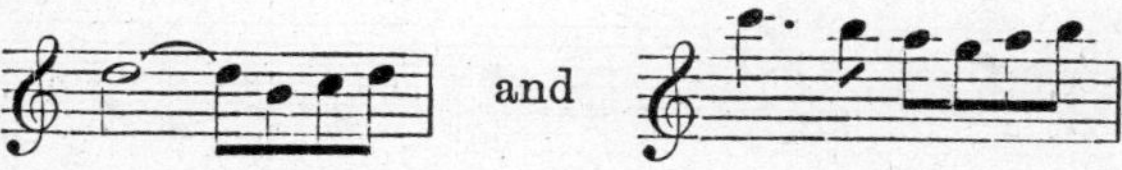

By our consideration of this extract we are brought naturally to a point at which it is easy to realize the great importance in a composer's scheme of the idea of repetition in some form or another. Here we see one aspect of it; in bars 5–9, this figure—

The element of Repetition.

is repeated four times, each time at a different pitch. This transposition, or shifting of the locality of a fragment of melody, and so changing its character, forms what is usually known as a Sequential passage or *Sequence.* Here it is the melody only which is so transposed; but sometimes, as in bars 10–13, the repetition is carried out more or less exactly in all the parts of the harmony. In the first case we have merely a Melodic sequence, whereas in the second case a Harmonic sequence is produced. Such sequences are of frequent occurrence in music; here are two further instances :—

Sequence.

(a) *Melodic Sequence.* BACH.—Prelude in C♯ minor, from 48 Preludes and Fugues.

(b) *Harmonic Sequence.* BEETHOVEN.—P.F. Sonata in A♭ (Op. 26).

Imitation. Another phase of repetition in music is shewn when one voice or part announces a "figure" or fragment of melody, and this is taken up by another voice or part, forming what is called an *Imitation*, *e.g.*:—

BEETHOVEN.—"Eroica" Symphony.

In the above example it will be seen that the figure of five notes given out first by the Flute and 1st Violins is *imitated* in bars 3—5 by the 2nd Violins, and then again by the 'Cellos and Double-basses in bars 5—7.

But there is yet a third and extremely important kind of repetition which is formed by the re-statement of a portion of a melody (or even of an extended composition) after a period of digression or contrast. If the reader will play or sing the following tune, he will readily perceive that the section marked A seems, as it were, to make a statement, to lay down a proposition; that at B to make a temporary digression from this—which, nevertheless, is in keeping with A; while the return to the first idea, in the passage indicated by A², seems to "round off" and to complete the whole in a manner that answers to our sense of fitness and balance:—

Repetition after digression.

Old Scotch Tune:—"Charlie is my darling."

By this three-fold design, which may be expressed by the following diagram:—

A	B	A²
Statement.	Digression or Contrast.	Re-statement.

the composer produces an effect both of Unity and of Diversity; unity by the coming back to his original statement towards the close of his composition, thus impressing us with the importance and significance of his principal thought; diversity by the temporary digression from this, supplied by the middle section, with its more or less contrasted nature. The force of what has been said will be evident either by omitting the middle

Unity and Diversity.

section of the tune, B, or by causing the music to cease at the termination of this middle section. In the first case the life and impulse of the piece would be ruined, for the reason that the very desire for the re-statement of A would be wanting; in the second case, the cessation of the music at the end of B would leave us entirely unconvinced, owing to the absence at that point of any feeling of completion or conclusiveness.

From our consideration of these various phases of repetition in music, we are able to see with tolerable clearness the importance, in the development of a musical idea, of in some way reproducing that idea under varied conditions, without destroying its identity. In other words, as was stated on page 10: amidst all the changes of character and feeling that are brought about by the composer's treatment of his theme, we are to realize that it is *still that same theme* which is the germ or seed from which so much has grown.

Power of developing musical ideas, a comparatively late product of musical art.

It must not be supposed that this power of developing musical themes without destroying their identity was arrived at early in the history of our art. By no means; it took literally centuries to discover these devices that seem to us so simple and so natural. If we go back to primitive times, or take the musical attempts of savage races to-day, we find that—as Sir Hubert Parry says in his "Art of Music"—"the primitive man lacks the power to think consecutively . . . His phrases are necessarily very short and their order unsystematic. It would be quite a feat for the aboriginal brain . . . to get even two . . . phrases to balance in an orderly manner."

The music of savage races.

So the savage goes on repeating over and over again, like a child, some simple and rude figure such as:—

Or, a little higher in the scale of humanity, perhaps we may find just a suggestion of contrast, thus:—

From such rude attempts to even the simplest folk-song of the more civilized nations is a long step indeed, and the power of continuity of thought had to grow enormously before we could have the delightful balance of phrase and the simple shapeliness of such a tune as "Barbara Allen."* Repetition,

* Quoted on page 20.

it will be seen, enters into the scheme both of the crude savage tune and of the beautiful folk-song—repetition even of small fragments of melody. But what a world of difference there is between the two! How charmingly the feeling of unity, of "family relationship," is maintained by the reproduction in fresh guises of the opening figure of "Barbara Allen"—

"Family relationship" between the various parts of a tune.

sometimes ascending and sometimes descending, but always with just sufficient variety in the outline to give the requisite feeling of diversity, and to produce a perfectly artistic result.

In future chapters we shall follow out the application of those principles of musical construction to which attention has already been drawn. These play such a notable part in the scheme of almost every kind of composition, from the simple folk-song or dance to the Beethoven Symphony, that it is of the highest importance that the listener should become acquainted with them in such a way that the many interesting and beautiful points of detail—which the composer surely means us to hear—shall not pass him by unappreciated and indeed unheeded, as so often is the case.

CHAPTER IV.

THE MATERIAL AND FORM OF INSTRUMENTAL COMPOSITION.

WHEN composers began, in the latter half of the 16th century and the early part of the 17th, to turn their attention to the writing of instrumental music, they found themselves face to face with the problem of how to continue and expand their ideas without the help of words. Before they could arrive at a purely instrumental style of writing in any way successful in character, many experiments had to be made and many failures registered.

It is necessary to remember that the vocal music which had been, and was then being, written for the Church rested its claim upon a "contrapuntal" or "polyphonic" style—a style, that is, in which each voice-part was equally important. The music flowed on and on without the rhyming periods familiar to us to-day; interest was kept up by

Old Church music and its style.

the constant, and at times somewhat artificial, use of imitational and other scientific devices. The following passage will illustrate just a little of the serene beauty of the best examples of this school of thought. It will doubtless be noticed that its lofty and passionless dignity well befits the text to which it is set :—

WILLIAM BYRD (1538–1623).—"Sanctus" from Mass for four voices.

Much choral music, too, of a secular type, such as Madrigals, Canzonas, etc., was written in this same contrapuntal style, and we find that these early composers often wrote music for instruments which might just as well have been sung by voices. Indeed, many of their pieces were, in England, published with the additional recommendation that they were "apt for voyces or for viols." The effect of these, without words and the tones of the human voice, was frequently very aimless, dull, and absolutely lacking in point, and men soon found out that some other method would have to be adopted if instrumental music was to strike out a path of its

Madrigals.

Early attempts at instrumental writing.

own and become interesting,* not to say intelligible, without the aid of words. But, for the moment, they were more or less groping in the dark; difficulties of which we have little idea faced them on all sides, and put them, in a sense, in the position of a mariner without a compass, with only a few dim and flickering stars to guide him on his way. Then it was that these early writers began to see in the simple and clear-cut rhythm of the "music of the people"—in the folk-songs and dances which had been growing up side by side with the more scientific music of the Church—a means by which they might evolve some sort of design to help them in making their instrumental compositions more shapely and coherent.

Folk-songs and dances.

From what has been said in the foregoing chapter it will have been gathered that these "people's tunes" were very simple in structure, and that their rhythm was for the most part clear even to squareness. It was just this clearness of shape that really gave composers their most valuable opportunity for the building-up and developing of a purely instrumental art, and history shews us that the first really successful instrumental pieces were in the form of dances—in character very like those of the people—but, as time went on, put together more and more artistically.† Amongst

People's tunes simple in rhythm.

* In Vol. III of "Burney's History of Music" the following quaint passage occurs *apropos* of this: "About the beginning of the 17th century," it runs, "Madrigals, which were almost the only compositions for the chamber then cultivated, seem to have been suddenly supplanted in the favour of lovers of music by a passion for *Fantasias* of 3, 4, 5 or 6 parts, wholly composed for viols and other instruments, without vocal assistance. And this passion seems to have arisen from the calling-in these instruments to reinforce the voice-parts with which they played in unison, in the performance of motets and madrigals. . . . At length, the instrumental performers discovered that both the poetry and singing of the times might be spared without any great loss or injury to musical effects; as the words, if good, were rendered unintelligible by fugue, imitation, and multiplicity of parts; and the singing, being often coarse and out of tune, could be better supplied by their own performance. Thus vocal music not only lost its independence, but was almost totally driven out of society: as the ancient Britons, calling in the Saxons to assist them in their conflicts with the Picts, were themselves subdued and forced from their possessions by too powerful auxiliaries."

† Considering the very inadequate nature of the instruments at their command, it is remarkable to find how much interest these old composers were able at times to impart to their music. For we must remember that the only keyed-instruments—beside the organ—were the old spinets‡ and virginals‡ of our forefathers, capable of little more than an amiable "tinkle," with absolutely no power of tone-contrast; that it was forbidden to use the thumb or little finger in organ-playing; and that all sorts of disabilities, of which we have little or no idea, were hampering these men in their efforts. Small wonder is it that the progress of purely instrumental art was at first laborious and slow!

‡ *See* Glossary.

such dances are to be found the Allemande, the Courante the Sarabande and the Gigue, together with others, such as the Gavotte, the Bourrée, the Minuet, the Pavan, the Galliard, etc., and very soon men began to arrange these in sets called "Suites" in Italian, "Ordres" in French, "Partitas' in German, and "Lessons" in English. These sets of dances reached their highest expression in the harpsichord* works of Bach and Handel in the earlier part of the 18th century.

Suites of dances.

Since then—from the time of Haydn and Mozart onwards—instrumental music has made great strides in independence of character and power of expression; but it must be remembered that such things as Sonatas, Symphonies, Concertos, and the many different present-day forms have in reality become possible through the older composers gradually realizing the value of rhythm, which revealed itself to them first in the traditional songs and dances.

Importance of rhythm.

When the old Suites had given place to the more modern types of instrumental art, we still find a survival of the old dance-forms in the Minuet, which—in the writings of Haydn and Mozart, and even of Beethoven—frequently occurs as one of the middle movements of a Sonata or a Symphony. Curiously, it is only the Minuet that has been so retained, the more regular constituents of the old Suites—such as the Allemande, Courante, Sarabande, and Gigue—having become purely things of the past, except in certain works of a special nature, where the composer may wish, perhaps, to impart an antique flavour to the music—possibly in connexion with some dramatic situation.

Survival of the Minuet in the modern Sonata or Symphony.

The Classic Minuet.

The Minuet has an importance in our study of the way in which composers build up their compositions, far beyond the fact of its survival as a link with the past. For, by its means, we can trace in a quite unique manner the principles that have guided men in the planning of many a work of large extent and noble aim. Some of these principles will be well illustrated by one or two examples. The first we shall consider is a Minuet from a "Suite de pièces," by Handel (1685–1759). In Handel's time, the Minuet was a slow and stately dance in $\frac{3}{4}$ time, somewhat dignified in character and style:—

The growth of the classic Minuet.

---

* *See* Glossary.

Molto moderato. HANDEL.—Minuet in F, from "Sept pièces."

In shape, it will be noticed, this Minuet does not—as do most modern compositions—divide itself into three parts, in the manner described on pages 25–26, but consists of two main sections, A and B. If the reader will refer to the Old English tune, "Barbara Allen," quoted on page 20, he will see that, in construction, the two pieces are—allowing for difference in size—practically identical. The two main sections of the Minuet are in the nature of Statement and Response, the first starting out from the tonic key and reaching the dominant at the double-bar, the second—after several incidental changes of key—duly concluding in the tonic. This particular musical form was almost exclusively adopted by the 17th and early 18th century composers, and is usually termed Binary (*i.e.*, two-part) form.

Two-part form of the old dances.

Even a casual examination of Handel's Minuet will reveal the fact that the second part is a good deal longer than the first. This is often the case with such pieces; after the composer has stated his main idea in a more or less concise way he frequently gives rein to his fancy in Part II, and enlarges upon any figure or fragment of melody which seems to suggest development. Two striking instances of this occur in the present example; in the first place the section marked (*a*) (*a*) in bars 9–10 is repeated exactly, in rising sequence, in bars 11–12; and again, with some slight modification, in bars 13–14, the repetition imparting a distinct element of zest and impetus to the music. Then again, a little later on, we find that Handel continues the melody of bars 17–18 (marked (*b*) (*b*)) by a similar sequential extension in bars 19–20,—this time making the repetition at a lower pitch.

Details of Handel's Minuet in F.

The conscious recognition of incidents such as these and many others, constitutes one very important step towards intelligent listening to music; in time—if we make the effort—the mind absorbs such points of detail easily and naturally as facts of value, and our enjoyment of what we may be hearing becomes more rational, for the reason that we are then *following what the composer means us to hear*, and are not allowing the music to reach us merely as a vague physical sensation.

Our next example is from Mozart (1756–1791). It is the 2nd Minuet (or Trio)* from the Symphony in E flat, No. 3, and shews us the changed character of the dance at this later period in the history of the art of music. The two great contemporary musicians, Haydn and Mozart, when they incorporated the Minuet into the scheme of their Sonatas and

A Mozart Minuet.

* *See* page 44.

Symphonies, quickened its pace to a considerable extent, and in their hands it loses much of the dignity of the older type, but gains an added life and animation. The Minuets of Mozart are mostly distinguished by a peculiar grace and charm of style, recognized by musicians as essentially his own; those of Haydn exhibiting a geniality, a directness, and an element of humour and fun which, again, are characteristics which we associate in a special degree with the writings of this particular master.

Changed character.

Let us listen to Mozart first:—

MOZART.—Symphony in E♭ (No. 3).

The first thing that strikes the attentive hearer is the utterly different impression left on the mind by this Minuet as compared with that by Handel quoted on page 31; here, in place of the almost austere stateliness of the earlier master, all is of an engaging and naïve simplicity, and the music flows along with the tranquillity of some gentle stream, with scarcely a ruffle on its surface. The construction of the piece presents some points worthy of our attention. In the first place we have here the three-fold design which was first introduced to our notice in connexion with the Scotch tune, "Charlie is my darling" (page 25). The piece divides itself into three parts (indicated in the example by the letters A—B—A^2), which respectively carry out the ideas of Statement, Digression and Re-statement. In the first eight bars Mozart announces the principal idea of the composition; the next eight, with their slightly more earnest character, expand that idea, afford the necessary element of variety, and—by modulating to another key (the dominant)—create a desire for the return to the original thought in the bar marked A^2, the last section, therefore, "rounding off" and completing the whole.

The Three-part form of the Mozart Minuet.

Points of imitation.

One other feature of this Minuet deserves notice, namely, the imitation in bars 4–5 of the figure in the melody of bars 3–4:—

and the similar imitation in bars 8—9 of the figure in bars 7–8:—

In the example as it is quoted above, this imitation appears in each case at the distance of an octave below, for convenience of playing on the Pianoforte; in the orchestral score it is actually in the same pitch, but of a different quality of tone. The figure is first given out by the Clarinet, and then answered by the Flute, thus:—

and similarly with the point in bars 7–9, both with delightful effect.

Our example from Haydn (1732–1809) will bring before us some further matters of importance. As to its life and "go," there can be no doubt; but over and above its special and individual character, it is on its constructive side particularly full of interest:—

A Haydn Minuet.

HAYDN.—Symphony in D (No. 2).

20
21
22
23
(a)
A²
24
sf
25
sf
26
f
27
28
29
30
31
32
33
34
tr
CODA.
tr
tr
35
36 sf
37-38
2
39
40

Besides providing another excellent instance of the three-part (or Ternary) form, the above Minuet is a notable illustration of the development of an entire composition from one or two small "figures." If we examine the piece from beginning to end, we shall find that two such "figures"—

Important "figures."

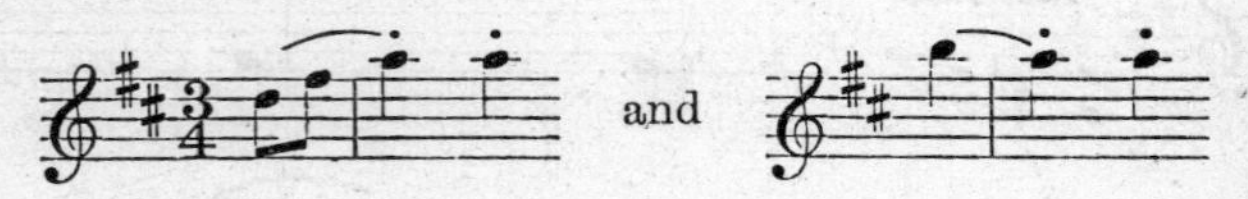

form the staple of the whole fabric. Not only is the melody of Part I evidence of this, but in Part II the same two figures are consistently "worked." The transference of the first of these to the bass part in bars 12–17, with a descending scale forming a counterpoint* against it, and the persistent use of both figures throughout the passage marked | (a) (a) | —gradually leading back to the re-entry of the opening phrase as Part III—should be most carefully noticed, as proof of the composer's power of "sticking to his subject," while at the same time he invests it with a continual freshness and variety of effect.

Concentration of aim.

Here, clearly, Haydn has solved the problem of the attainment of diversity within unity, that problem which was destined to be solved in an even more remarkable manner by his great successor, Beethoven.

To return, however, to the consideration of the Minuet: the passage at | (a) (a) | was referred to just now as one that led back to the original idea at the opening of Part III. The music had arrived, in bar 18, at a perfect cadence in the key of the dominant, viz. A major, and of course gives us the impression of being "away from home"—so to speak. From this point the composer wishes to return to his original key, D major, and he effects his purpose most artistically by eight

Further points of interest.

* *See* Glossary.

bars upon a dominant pedal,* over which the original figures of the piece appear in guises such as the following :—

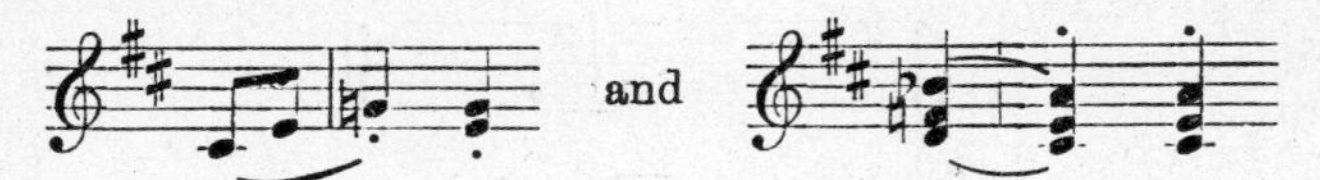

the former of these afterwards being elaborated, in bars 22, 23, into—

Here the two figures are set one against the other in an ingenious manner :—

passing without break into the resumption of the original phrase in the original key. The initial figure retains its elaborated form, and assumes by that means an added gaiety which imparts a sense of increasing exhilaration to the music :—

This exhilaration is heightened by the way in which Haydn terminates the whole piece. It will be seen that the re-statement of Part I is complete in bar 34, but that the cadence here is less decisive than in the first instance. Compare bars 7 and 8 :—

* *See* Glossary.

where the sentence finishes on the key-note in the melody, with bars 33 and 34 :—

with the melody ending upon the third of the scale. Haydn makes this change in order that he may carry the piece further, and so add what is known as a *Coda*,* by way of a final climax to the whole. This he does by transposing the chords last quoted into another key, and then—after two bars of silence, as unexpected as humorous—by repeating the perfect cadence in the tonic key with additional emphasis, thus :—

The Coda.

again repeating it in the four last bars against the two original figures, thus "driving home" his main thought effectively and brilliantly.

Of the importance in music of the Coda there will be many occasions to speak in later chapters of this volume ; the above example will abundantly demonstrate its purpose for the present.

The simple three-part structure exemplified in the two Minuets from Mozart and Haydn (which is conveniently expressed by the formula A—B—A²) is the basis of most of the smaller pieces of composers of all schools of thought.

The Three-part form now almost universal in some way or other.

It is in such cases well-nigh universal, as may easily be seen by reference to the Minuets of the classical masters, the simpler "Lieder ohne Worte" of Mendelssohn, many of the pieces in Schumann's "Album for the Young," the "Lyrische Stückchen" of Grieg, etc., etc.

* "Coda": *lit.* a "tail-piece."

Presently we shall see that this three-part (or Ternary) form underlies other and far more extended works than the slight pieces we have been hitherto discussing.

The "musical sandwich."

Upon the root-idea of the "musical sandwich," as it has been humorously described, most of the important modern designs such as the Sonata, the Symphony and the Concerto are built up. As we shall realize from future examples, this form is capable of infinite expansion, and of endless variety of detail; and it is this fact, coupled with a certain reasonableness in the idea of a return to an original proposition after a temporary digression, that has caused it to be fruitful in results in so many directions.

CHAPTER V.

THE LARGER DESIGNS IN MUSIC.

Before we proceed to a detailed consideration of works larger and more complex than those we have hitherto had under review, it will be well to take stock -so to speak—of the various ways in which a composer proceeds when he wishes to write something bigger, longer, and more important.* Three main avenues are open to him:—

The "secondary character" in the musical story.

1. He may add to an existing piece of comparatively small dimensions, another of *contrasted idea and key*, at the conclusion of which he will return to the first, and re-state it—most probably in its entirety. It will readily occur to the mind of the reader that the introduction of a new and contrasted theme in the middle stimulates the listener, by affording the necessary variety which a longer design demands. In other words, it brings a "secondary character" into the story—just as in a novel or a play—by which interest in the principal theme is enhanced, and a desire set up in the mind for its ultimate return, to be carried to its fulfilment and proper climax.

---

* We shall not, for reasons of space, deal in this volume with contrapuntal designs like the Fugue, neither can we discuss the construction of vocal works. For a consideration of the subject of Fugue the reader is referred to the author's "Form in Music." (Joseph Williams, Ltd.)

The "ground-plan" of such a composition will be clearly shewn by the following diagram:—

I	II	III
Principal Theme, in the tonic key, usually complete in itself, and often consisting of the now familiar A—B—A² design.	Theme of Contrast, in some other key—at times complete in itself, like the Principal Theme.	Return of Principal Theme, in the tonic key—frequently in its entirety. This is often followed by a Coda.

The most obvious illustration of this type of form is the Minuet and Trio of the classical masters, the Trio* being the theme of contrast coming between the two presentations of the Minuet; but countless examples are to hand in the many Marches, Polonaises, Mazurkas, Romances, Impromptus, Nocturnes, and other "fugitive pieces" written for the Pianoforte, and also in the slighter movements of Sonatas and Symphonies.†

The theme of contrast.

2. He may retain the original three-part or Ternary form, but expand each of its parts to a much larger size—filling each part fuller, as it were—consequently making a greater demand upon the attention of the listener, by reason of the greater continuity of the music. When such is the case, the composer has still to allow for the element of contrast necessary in a long work—but in another way from that just mentioned. He attains this by dividing the music of Part I (A) into two portions, contrasted in key and in character. In other words, Part I contains two different themes or *subjects* which, on the re-statement of (A) as Part III, generally recur *in one and the same key*, viz. that of the tonic. The middle part (B), in such pieces, develops or expands either or both of these themes in various ways. The type of movement thus produced is that almost always used for the first movement of a Sonata or a Symphony, and is usually described as *Sonata-form*, or *First-movement form*.

Sonata-form.

The following diagram will, it is hoped, make this particular design clear to the mind:—

---

* *See* page 44.

† When two or more such themes of contrast separate various appearances of the Principal Theme, we have the type of composition known as the Rondo.

A	B	A²
(i) First Theme, or Subject, in the tonic key, leading to— (ii) Second Theme, or Subject, in a contrasted key, often that of the dominant.	Expansion or Development of either or both of these Themes, through various keys, and in many guises.	(i) First Theme, or Subject, in the tonic key, followed by— (ii) Second Theme, or Subject, this time transposed into the tonic key. *Coda.*

The Exposition, Development and Recapitulation of Sonata-form.

In Sonatas and similar works, A is usually called the *Exposition, i.e.*, the part which "places forth," or sets out in order, the main ideas of the movement, which the composer will afterwards develop and discuss. The second part, B, is described either as the *Development*, or the *Free Fantasia*,* for the reason already explained; the third part, A², being referred to as the *Recapitulation*, because in this part a recapitulation or re-statement of the first part takes place. This re-statement, as will be seen later, is not always exact, or even complete; but it always brings back enough of the opening part to produce that feeling of roundness and of symmetry to which reference has already been made.

Variations on a theme.

3. He may take some short theme, either in a two-part form (such as "Barbara Allen"), or a three-part form (such as "Charlie is my darling" or the Mozart Minuet on page 33), and immediately re-state the whole of it under different conditions, embellishing it and disguising it from time to time in such a way that its repetition shall not become wearisome to the listener, but always maintain the necessary feeling of interest in his mind. When the composer works upon his original idea in this manner, he is said to write *Variations* on that theme. As we shall see later, this type of art has suffered from time to time from a vulgar and inartistic use of some of its more obvious and easily-debased features. In the hands of the great masters, however, this "Variation form" has served, and still serves, as the basis of some of their most expressive and artistic writings, and thus gives proof, if proof were needed, of its inherent vitality.

---

* Because the composer here gives rein to his fancy (Fantasia = fancy) in the expansion and treatment of his subjects.

CHAPTER VI.

THE MINUET AND TRIO AS A TYPE OF FORM—THE "THEME OF CONTRAST."

In the preceding chapter, in speaking of the various ways in which a composer is enabled to expand the size of his work beyond the limits of the very concise pieces treated of previously, it was stated that the Minuet and Trio of the classical masters afforded a very familiar and easily-comprehended illustration of one method by which he could accomplish his purpose. It is important to remember that it was the custom from fairly early times in the history of instrumental music to follow the playing of a Minuet, a Gavotte, a Bourrée, or other such dance, by a *second* of somewhat contrasted character, after which the first was played over again. Most of the earliest instances of this proceeding shew us the second dance written in three-part harmony—usually for two viols and a bass. As a consequence, the term "Trio" came to be used as a frequent description of this second dance; and, somewhat curiously, has been retained in this connexion, although the practice of writing this particular piece in three-part harmony has long since died out.*

The "Trio."

A moment's thought will reveal the fact that in the plan of the Minuet and Trio we have in substance the idea conveyed by the diagram on page 42, and we shall see presently that from this composers have been able to arrive at a form suitable for pieces of very divergent character.

Minuet and Trio form.

Our first illustration of this kind of design is the Scherzo and Trio from Beethoven's Pianoforte Sonata in A flat (Op. 26). We have chosen this in preference to an actual *Minuet* and Trio for two reasons: firstly, because the form itself is precisely the same, and, secondly, because the "Scherzo," as seen in the works of Beethoven, is the direct lineal descendant of the Minuets of Mozart and Haydn, of which examples have already been given. When these two masters incorporated the Minuet into the scheme of their Symphonies, etc., its speed was increased and its character underwent a change—as was shewn on pages 32–33; the dignity and stateliness observable in the

The "Scherzo," its origin.

---

* The second of two Gavottes was often called a Musette, from the fact that it was generally written upon a "drone" bass, in imitation of the *Musette* or bagpipe.

older Minuets of Handel, Bach and others gave way before the geniality of Haydn and the grace of Mozart. When, in the course of time, Beethoven began to build on the foundation laid by these masters, the Minuet became—by reason of yet another considerable quickening of its "tempo"—modified out of all recognition. Its relationship to the original classic dance was in this way so obscured that the designation "Minuet" was no longer appropriate to express the newer spirit of the movement, and Beethoven soon abandoned it in favour of the title "Scherzo,"* which was much more in keeping with the vigour, the restless activity, and the often unbridled humour displayed in the most characteristic examples of his writing.

The Scherzo from the Op. 26 Sonata, though hardly exhibiting these qualities so markedly as the Scherzos, for example, in the third, fifth, and ninth Symphonies, yet gives us more than one glimpse of those *traits* which we especially associate with the genius of Beethoven.

Let us take note of its "motto-theme," from which almost everything in the movement springs :—

What a world of difference there is between this and the opening of the Handel Minuet, quoted on page 31! A new era has dawned, and Music is speaking with a different voice, is delivering a different message—a message whose individuality and independence are revealed to us in progressive measure throughout the long chain of the master's works.

The newer spirit revealed in the Scherzos of Beethoven.

The following is an outline sketch of the Scherzo, which is in Ternary, or Three-part, form :—

* *Lit.* = a jest.

(Then succeed
8 bars consisting
of a varied
repetition of the
preceding.)
B
p
(Here Beethoven expands, or
develops, his original idea.)
f
sf
p
f
sf
p
f
sf
sf
p
(This figure
is then
repeated for
7 more bars.)
pp

* When two parts of the harmony are invertible in this way, they are said to be in Double Counterpoint with each other.

CODA.
sf
sf
cres.
ff
TRIO (or theme of contrast).
A
p sempre legato.
cres.
sf
p
B
p
cres.

The Scherzo, as will be seen by the foregoing quotation, is succeeded by the Trio, or theme of contrast. The Scherzo and Trio are both self-contained movements; either of them could, in reality, exist separately. Placed as they are, though, and played in succession, without break, each forms a foil to the other, and heightens its interest; the return of the Scherzo at the conclusion of the Trio coming with a natural and welcome sense of fitness and completeness which the mind instinctively realizes and appreciates.

Scherzo and Trio independent as to form.

The Trio is in D flat major, the sub-dominant key, and consists of only *two* parts, being therefore in Binary form. In character it is in entire contrast with the Scherzo, being gentle and tranquil by reason of its undulating figure, which is maintained throughout with delightful effect.

The artistic way in which Beethoven prepares us for the return of the Scherzo by the four bars at (*a*) founded upon its "motto-theme," and forming a kind of link or passage of transition between the two, should not escape the reader's attention.

A link to unite the Trio with the return of the Scherzo.

The direction in Italian, at this point, signifies that the Scherzo is to be played over again from the beginning (*Da Capo*), but without the repetition of B and A² which is indicated by the dots after the first double-bar. It should be noticed, in passing, that it was—and often still is—the custom for the different parts of such small pieces as Gavottes, Minuets, Scherzos, etc., to be repeated. When this happens, Part I (A) is repeated by itself, Parts II and III (B and A²) being repeated without a break between them. After the digression caused by the Trio, when the original piece is played again, these "repeat-marks" are disregarded.

Our next example will shew us this particular musical form—in which two distinct and self-contained themes, each to all intents and purposes complete in itself, are placed in contrast with each other—adopted as the structural basis of a composition of an utterly different kind as regards character and expression. It will be noticed that in this instance the ideas are more closely woven together; there is less definite separation of the two contrasting themes, which here are linked up with one another so as to form a more continuous whole:—

The Minuet and Trio form used for other classes of composition.

Molto vivace. CHOPIN.—Valse in D flat.

2nd.

* This Theme of Contrast is, unusually, in the same key as the Principal Theme.

tr
Dal Segno.
Principal Theme here returns, and is repeated substantially as before, beginning at the sign 𝄋, and continuing until the point marked FINE.

CHAPTER VII.

THE SONATA OR SYMPHONY—ITS FIRST MOVEMENT.

Experiments in musical design.

EVER since the time when the old suites of dances represented the highest point to which instrumental music had attained on its road of independent existence, composers had been making various experiments in musical form; but it was left more particularly to Carl Philip Emanuel Bach, a son of the great Johann Sebastian, to point the way by which the art of instrumental writing might travel on this road of independence with a rapidity unrealized before his time.

Carl Philip Emanuel Bach.

Upon the foundation laid by him, his great successors, Haydn and Mozart, were enabled to perfect that structural design which has since formed the basis of so many works of importance. We refer to Sonata-form,* or First-movement form which, in its three-fold idea of Exposition, Development and Recapitulation (page 43), carries out on a larger and more exalted scale the principle of construction embodied in the formula A—B—A^2.

Sonata-form.

Before describing this more in detail, and shewing how composers have worked upon it, it is necessary to say a few words in general about the important class of instrumental works known as Sonatas, Symphonies, etc.

Sonata and Symphony.

The words Sonata and Symphony are met with in the writings of the early instrumental composers as the titles of complete works, or of single movements in complete works; but it is essential that we should remember that, in such cases, these terms imply something very different from their modern use. Indeed, such expressions as Symphony, Concerto, Overture, and Sonata, although now representing works of special and particular character, were used quite loosely to describe practically one and the same idea—merely that of a composition for an instrument or instruments, as opposed to one for voices.†

It is impossible, in the limits of the present volume, to trace the gradual narrowing-down of these terms, each to its own individual signification; neither can we pass in review the

* This term, it should be remembered, does not refer to the shape of the *Sonata as a whole*, but only to that of one of its movements, usually the first. (*See* page 42.)

† In this connexion, it is interesting to note that the term *Sonata* (*i.e.*, "played") was often used as the antithesis of *Cantata* (*i.e.*, "sung") —the former to indicate a composition for an instrument, the latter one for a solo-voice.

several interesting stages in the historical development of the Sonata-form, important as they are. We must content ourselves for the present with saying that the modern Sonata and Symphony practically date from the period of Haydn and Mozart, and that, although we frequently find the words employed by J. S. Bach, and even earlier, by Corelli and others, the works so entitled by these composers present little, either of form or of character, which musicians associate with works similarly designated, written at a later date.

The modern Sonata and Symphony date from the period of Haydn and Mozart.

A Sonata, nowadays, may be described as a composition for a solo instrument, or for two instruments in combination, having two or more separate movements (usually three or four), so arranged as to form a well-balanced whole. To afford the requisite element of diversity, these movements are contrasted with one another in speed and style. Thus, if a Sonata consists of three movements (as do many of those of the classical masters), the first is generally an *Allegro* of somewhat important scope, the second a slow movement of an expressive or tender nature, and the *Finale* another quick movement. If a Sonata has four movements, the additional one is most frequently either a *Minuet and Trio*, or a *Scherzo and Trio*, whose usual place is between the slow movement and the Finale.

Description of a Sonata.

It was stated above that the term Sonata applies only to a composition either for one instrument, or for two. So far as the actual use of the term goes, this is really the case; but there are very many works which, though not so described, are in fact Sonatas in all but name. Trios, Quartets, Quintets, etc., for stringed or wind instruments are merely Sonatas for three, four, five, or more such instruments; a Symphony is an orchestral Sonata; while a Concerto is a Sonata in which a solo instrument, such as the pianoforte or violin, is associated—in a specially prominent manner—with the orchestra.* There seems little reason for the change of name in most of these cases; but the practice gradually grew up, and as in so many similar instances, custom has sanctioned what is in reality a somewhat absurd anomaly.

Other works that are in reality Sonatas, though not so designated.

Since Haydn's day, it has been the habit of composers —when writing works on the plan of the Sonata—to cast one movement at least in the special form or shape known as *Sonata-form* (*see* pages 42 and 43). In the great majority of instances it is the opening "Allegro" which corresponds to this specia

First-movement form.

* An *Overture* is usually on the plan of the first movement of a Sonata.

design,* and this fact has led to the use of the alternative expression, "First-movement-form."

We have already gathered that this form is an amplified and exalted version of the A—B—A² plan of musical construction, a version in which the first part (A) is subdivided into two portions, called respectively the First Subject and the Second Subject. These subjects, or themes, are in contrasted keys—often the tonic and dominant, but not always—and usually present some distinctiveness of character. Very frequently—but, again, not invariably—the First Subject is stronger, more pithy, more striking, in the manner of its presentation than its companion theme; it usually consists of some sharply defined figure which impresses itself on our attention and our memory, and from which, as from a seed, much that follows in the course of the movement will in all probability germinate and develop. Listen to the following typical "First Subject" figures:—

First and Second Subjects.

Typical First Subjects.

* But by no means invariably; it is the *last* movement of Beethoven's Sonata (Op. 27, No. 2), for example, which is in this particular form, not the first.

The Second Subject.

The Second Subject in a well-written work brings in the element of variety; although in keeping with the First Subject, it usually exhibits some change of mood, and in many instances is more in the nature of an extended melody, *e.g.*:—

In the earlier specimens of Sonata-writing, such as are represented by many of the works of the period of Haydn and Mozart, these two subjects were somewhat markedly cut off from one another, often by intervening sections of slight musical value, which seemed to do little more than "mark time"—so to speak—until the entrance of something of greater importance and worth. Bustling scale-passages and formal broken-chord figures heralded the expected new theme, in a manner

Conventional passage-writing.

somewhat trite and meaningless to modern ears, causing Wagner to compare them—in a now historic phrase—to "the clatter of dishes between the courses at a princely banquet."*

Here are some typical specimens:—

* In allusion to the positions held by Haydn and Mozart in the households of the Archdukes and Archbishops of the day, under whose patronage they lived and worked.

We must remember, however, that such conventional passages of transition as these, and endings like the following:—

MOZART.—Sonata in C (No. 8).

though seemingly of little musical interest, served a distinct purpose at the time at which they were written. Sonata-form was a new and unfamiliar design, and by such means as these the course of the movement was to some extent mapped out for the listener, who was thus enabled the more clearly to "find his way," and to follow the unfolding of the composer's plan with the greater ease and certainty.

The great service rendered to art by Haydn and Mozart.

In studying the writings of these pioneers of modern music, it is necessary to focus such matters aright in our minds, and to put them in their proper place in estimating the value of whatever work we have under consideration. There is always the danger lest—by being out of sympathy with certain incidents we may deem antiquated and conventional—we lose sight of surrounding beauties, or fail to recognize the immense importance of the labours of these "path-finders" of musical art. Through their efforts alone the foundations were laid upon which, in the course of time, such a marvellous superstructure has been built by Beethoven and his successors.

Analysis of a Sonata-movement by Beethoven.

We will now take a Sonata of Beethoven—that in G major (Op. 14, No. 2)—and comment on the plan of the Exposition of the first movement, by which it is hoped the reader will get some clear grasp of the principles that guide composers in this part of their work. Here is the outline of the Exposition, which should be supplemented by a reference to a copy of the complete Sonata :—

* *See* Glossary.

22
23
24
25
(Second Subject (a) in D major.)
(Second Subject (b))
41

42
43
(Second Subject (c))
(Codetta, or closing section of Exposition.)
tr

The foregoing Exposition is notable for several reasons; in the first place it shews us the importance in the composer's scheme of a striking and easily-remembered figure or idea, as the basis of his First Subject. In this particular instance—as we shall find later in considering the Development section—Beethoven makes constant use of the following "germ-thought":—

The importance of the "germ-idea."

creating it as the seed from which so much that is interesting and beautiful is to spring into being in the course of his design.

Contrast of subjects.

In the next place we see the needed contrast with this carried out in the different branches of the Second Subject,* with their more melodious and "tune-like" character:—

Then, how delightfully the transition between the First and Second Subjects is managed; the music merges easily and flowingly from the key and feeling of the one, to the key and feeling of the other. In bar 14 Beethoven almost imperceptibly begins to tend in key towards the dominant (D major), and in bar 19 a prolonged pedal-note† on the *dominant of* that dominant key prepares the mind for the appearance—after a rising scale-passage in bars 24 and 25—of the Second Subject. Here is no "padding"; all is germane to the matter in hand, and each bar seems truly the natural outcome of the bar that precedes it. Beethoven, with the experience of Haydn and Mozart before him, is enabled thus to make the

Transition between the subjects.

---

* The Second Subject frequently contains two or more separate musical ideas, which lead one into the other, as in the present Sonata.

† *See* Glossary.

whole structure "hang together" in a way which they only dimly foreshadowed, but which was rendered possible to the later master through the fact of their having hammered out *the main principles of the form*, which he afterwards was destined so lavishly to enrich.

Concluding section of Exposition.

Lastly, let us notice the artistic little "Codetta," or concluding section, of this Exposition. All it does from a structural standpoint is to emphasize the tonic and dominant chords of D major, the key of the Second Subject; but this is done without any of that parading of the fact we so often see in the older Sonatas. The formal purpose is achieved no less surely; but, again, we are made to feel how this is subordinated to the *musical* interest; the anatomy is perfect, but what we realize over and above all is the spirit that breathes through it, and makes it in truth a living thing :—

Repeat of Exposition.

It will be seen, on reference to a copy of this Sonata, that the Exposition—which terminates at the conclusion of this Codetta—is marked off from the music that follows by a double-bar with a "repeat-mark." With the pre-Beethoven writers this custom was practically universal, and the Exposition was almost always repeated, as it is here. This repetition had the undeniable advantage of impressing the subject-matter of the movement upon the listener's attention, and the practice is still adhered to in a good many modern works. Beethoven as a rule keeps to the old practice in the matter; but in a few of his later and more impassioned Sonatas, such as that in F minor (Op. 57), he dispenses with the "repeat," and the music undoubtedly gains in impulse by being allowed to proceed uninterruptedly to its development and final climax.

The Development section; its purpose.

The next incident in the course of a movement in Sonata-form is the Development-section or "Free Fantasia" (*see* the diagram on page 43). Here the composer subjects his themes to whatever changes of treatment his fancy and imagination suggest to him; they appear in many different guises and take on many different shades of feeling. Unexpected changes of key, fresh figures of accompaniment or of counterpoint, new and varied rhythms—all are laid under contribution to impart that quickening of the interest that attaches to the successful working-out of his story. We instinctively feel that "the plot thickens," as we are led step by step through the "pleasing bewilderment"* of this Development section to the final solution in the Recapitulation and the Coda.

Let us look a little closely into the Development of this particular Sonata of Beethoven. It begins with the "motto-figure" of the First Subject—this time in the minor mode:—

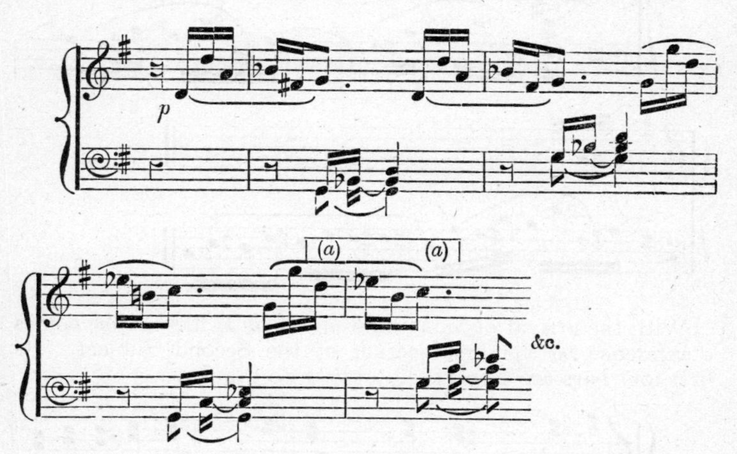

Varied rhythms.

Thus far the music follows the rhythm of the First Subject as it appears in the Exposition; but now Beethoven—with a sure instinct for variety and a perfect knowledge of the fact that development means something more than repetition—breaks away from this rhythm; and, by a delightful touch, carries on the original thought in an entirely new and unlooked-for way. He detaches the last four notes of the "motto-figure" (*see* | (a) (a) | above), and passes them from octave to octave against a steadily-descending bass, thus:—

* The late E. Dannreuther, in "Macmillan's Magazine."

Here we reach the dominant chord of the key of B flat major, and the "motto-figure" is treated in close imitation between the two hands, the left hand continuing the passage until the tonic of the key is reached:—

Effective imitation.

With the arrival of this tonic chord of B flat major, comes a reference to the first section of the Second Subject. Its first four bars are transposed intact into this key:—

Then, with no less art than was exhibited in the breaking of the rhythm of the First Subject at the commencement of the Development section, Beethoven insists upon the figure of this this Second Subject against a rising bass:—

Changed character of First Subject.

At this point the music which, up till now, has been gentle and persuasive in character, changes its mood, and a long passage of strength and vigour ensues. The "motto-theme" is given out, *forte*, in the bass, against a triplet accompaniment in the right hand. This is developed through the keys of A flat major, G minor, F minor and B flat major, until it comes to a pause upon the Dominant 7th chord in the key of E flat major. Reference should here be made to a copy of the Sonata; the following extract will, however, indicate the manner in which this particular passage—too long for quotation in its entirety—sets out:—

After the "pause" just referred to, the first four bars of the First Subject appear again, "piano," in the key of E flat, after which the figure occurring first in bar 5 of the whole movement, thus:—

is extended by sequence in an interesting manner:—

Beethoven here reaches a "Pedal"* upon the dominant of his original key, G major, and begins at once to prepare for the return of the First Subject at the beginning of the Recapitulation. Eight bars of rushing scale-passages (possibly having some connexion with those in the Exposition in bars 41–43) accompany a figure in the left hand which it is hardly too fanciful to imagine as being based upon the "motto-theme"—in notes of twice the original value (*see* | (a) (a) | :—

* *See* Glossary.

The approach to the First Subject in the Recapitulation.

In the transition into the Recapitulation, Beethoven gives an illustration of the old adage that "coming events cast their shadows before," for it is founded entirely upon the last four notes of the "motto":—

The repetitions of this fragment become closer and closer, causing the music to increase in earnestness and intensity:—

Then, still further to add to its impetus, the composer splits up this tiny figure yet again by means of "phrasing" it into groups of two notes—against the accent:—

Here again, in this transitional passage—just as in that between the First and Second Subjects—there is no "padding"; we see that the smallest and most insignificant figure with Beethoven often becomes of greatest importance in the working out of his purpose. "No musician"—says Sir Hubert Parry, in reference to Beethoven's "Development" sections, "ever had such capacity for throwing an infinite variety of lights upon a central idea; it is no 'business' or pedantry, but an extraordinary genius for transforming rhythms and melodies so that though they be recognized by the hearer as the same which he has heard before, they seem to tell a totally different story; just as the same ideas working in the minds of men of different circumstances or habits of thought may give them the most opposite feelings."

Importance of the smallest figure in Beethoven's scheme.

We now reach the third stage in the movement, viz. the Recapitulation, where the composer re-asserts his main ideas in their more complete shape, and by this means brings home to our minds a fuller sense of the meaning and intention of all that has been taking place in the section of Development. The Recapitulation in the Sonata before us, like those in most of the Sonatas of Beethoven's immediate predecessors, is—except for the fact that the Second Subject reappears in the *Tonic* key—practically an exact reproduction of the Exposition. The mere circumstance of this change of key, however, enables Beethoven to give us one of those delightful and subtle touches which, to the majority of listeners, are too often "as though they were not." It occurs in the course of the transition between the two main subjects, and consists in the introduction of three extra bars—in sequence with what has gone just before—modulating into C major in a peculiarly winning way:—

The Recapitulation.

Fresh points of beauty.

The object of this is that the music may reach the tonic key (G major) for the Second Subject, *from C major*, in the same way as the dominant key (D major) was reached, at a similar point in the Exposition, *from G major*. On reference to a copy of the Sonata, it will be seen that, from the point at which our last quotation ended, the course of the music is identical with that of the Exposition, save of course that it is all transposed a 4th higher, into the tonic key. The three separate divisions of the Second Subject recur in due order, the last of these terminating slightly differently, thus:—

The Coda.

The concluding section, or Codetta, does not reappear, but instead we have a *Coda** of some importance, founded upon the Principal Subject of the movement. Notice the tender "farewell" reminiscence of the motto-figure in the final bars:—

* Beethoven's Codas are always one of the most striking features of his work.

We have gone thus into detail with respect to this movement in order, first, to shew the reader what a number of beautiful and interesting points there are in such things which—it is not too much to say—often fail to reach the average hearer's mind in such a way that he realizes them consciously, or with any sense of true appreciation. Secondly, we have analysed this movement thus fully in order that he may be helped to "look beneath the surface" in the compositions with which he may be brought into contact, either in his own playing or when listening to the playing of others. Thus, and thus only, will he derive the highest enjoyment from the music which he hears, for he will then find himself following, in an active and interested way, that which the composer wishes him to hear, instead of allowing it all to pass him by in drowsy ignorance or passive indifference.

CHAPTER VIII.

THE REMAINING MOVEMENTS OF A SONATA OR SYMPHONY.

As the present volume does not in the first and foremost place profess to be a treatise on Musical Form, it is impossible for us to discuss with any degree of fulness or completeness the many interesting shapes or designs which are met with from time to time in the works of the great masters of music. It must suffice here to set forth a few general principles which may be some sort of guide to the listener, so that he may at least be prepared in some measure to "find his way," and within limits to know what to expect in the different sections of an important work.

The reader will doubtless remember that a composition of the nature and scope of a Sonata or a Symphony usually contains three, or four, separate movements, most frequently in the following order:—

The remaining movements of a Sonata or Symphony; their usual order.

(i) An "Allegro" in Sonata-form (or First-movement form, as it is sometimes called).

(ii) A slow movement of an expressive or lyrical character.

(iii) A Minuet and Trio, or a Scherzo and Trio (in four-movement works).

(iv) A final quick movement.

In the preceding chapter we have considered in detail the main features that usually present themselves to our notice in a first movement; it now remains to make some reference to the general characteristics of those that succeed it.

The Slow-movement; its function.

The slow movement of a Sonata or a Symphony in the great majority of instances comes next after the first movement, and presents a complete contrast to it. Whereas the opening "Allegro" has manifested the composer's powers of development, his constructive skill, and his ability—so to speak—to "think imperially" in music, the slow movement gives him the opportunity of shewing another and totally different aspect of his art. Here emotional expressiveness, tenderness and melodic charm hold sway, and in a very special sense it is the lyrical or song-like element that predominates. With Haydn and Mozart and their contemporaries the slow movement was the vehicle for the display of a considerable amount of engaging florid ornamentation in the melody. For the most part the themes of Beethoven's slow movements are embellished less in this particular way, and strike a deeper note of earnestness; indeed, it may be said that in no other part of his work is his individuality manifested more truly and remarkably.

The difference in character between the slow movements of Haydn and Mozart and those of Beethoven.

The difference in style and temper between a slow movement by Mozart and a Beethoven "Largo" will be readily perceived :—

Largo e mesto. BEETHOVEN.—Sonata in D (Op. 10, No. 3).

The extract from Mozart shews in a marked manner the "ornamented" nature of the melody, to which allusion has already been made. This particular style of writing was the natural outcome of the lack of sustaining power in the harpsichords and pianofortes of the day, upon which it was almost impossible to prolong the sounds in such a way that a slow, deeply expressive melody would be effective. This limitation did not hold, of course, in connexion with the instruments of the orchestra or the string-quartet, and the kind of florid writing in the passage we have quoted is not then met with quite to the same extent; although in many instances the prevalent fondness for ornament is still evident.

Mozart's ornamentation.

On referring to the extract from Beethoven, we shall notice an utter dissimilarity of style and feeling; there is an entire absence of embellishment and "embroidery," and the music derives its emotional power as much from the richness of its harmony as from the beauty of its slowly-moving melody. There is hardly anything more noteworthy in the history of musical art than the great advance in intimacy and depth of expression revealed by the writings of Beethoven, and the slow movements of his Sonatas, Quartets, and Symphonies are full of passages which are proof of the newer spirit of earnestness which was then making itself felt so unmistakably, and which was destined to yield such magnificent results.

Beethoven's richness of harmony.

The form of a slow movement varies from time to time; there is no one type of design that can be said to be associated with it as "Sonata-form" is with the first movement. Perhaps most frequently we find the form based upon that of the Minuet and Trio, thus:—

The form of slow movements.

I	II	III
Principal Theme (perhaps a complete A—B—A 2 design)—in tonic key.	Theme of Contrast (or "Episode") in some other key.	Re-statement of Principal Theme, and most probably a *Coda*.

Episodical form of the slow movement of Mendelssohn's Violin Concerto.

Of this there is a particularly good instance in the "Andante" of Mendelssohn's Violin Concerto. Its principal theme begins as follows:—

and, after being expanded to some length, is succeeded by the theme of contrast (or Episode), in the orchestra:—

which eventually leads back in a most artistic way into the return of the opening subject. This, on its repetition, is somewhat abbreviated, but is followed by a charming *Coda* of ten or a dozen bars bringing the movement to a peaceful conclusion.

The Rondo.

At times the *Rondo* form is used (see page 42); at others a somewhat modified and abridged kind of Sonata-form, and yet again the movement may take the shape of a *Theme and*

Variations. In this case, as we stated on page 43, the composer takes some simple complete theme, and repeats it several times under different conditions, with such elaborations and modifications as may serve to prevent these continued repetitions from becoming wearisome, and to bring out anything suggestive of development in the theme itself. Of such variations we have excellent examples in several of the Sonatas of Beethoven, *e.g.*, in the "Andante" of Op. 14, No. 2; the "Andante con variazioni" of Op. 26; the "Andante con moto" of Op. 57; the "Andante molto cantabile ed espressivo" of Op. 109, and the "Adagio molto" of Op. 111. The most familiar of these to most people is the "Andante" of Op. 26; it begins with the following well-known tune (in simple three-part form):—

The Theme and Variations.

Beethoven's Op. 26 Variations.

Variation 1 sets out with this figure—

which persists throughout, the harmonies by which it is supported being identical with those of the original theme.

In Variation 2 Beethoven shifts the melody to the bass, thus:—

In Variation 3 the mode changes from major to minor, and the melody of the theme is a good deal disguised, although the first two or three bars still suggest it:—

After this extremely expressive variation, the mode changes back again in Variation 4, which starts with the following new figure over a "staccato" bass—

continued throughout with delicate effect. In the final variation Beethoven returns to the outline of the original melody, but embellished and "embroidered" in triplet figures—

and then completes the whole movement with a tranquil Coda of sixteen bars, commencing thus:—

We have chosen the above illustration of Variation Form largely on account of the comparatively simple nature of the variations themselves. But in more elaborate examples of this kind of writing, the variations often depart far more widely from the melody of the theme, which in such cases just gives the composer a sort of text, suggestive of many different applications. Within the limits of a reasonable connexion with that text, the writer may present to us his own "commentary"—so to speak—upon any part of it; and a single figure will now and again furnish the basis of his operations. As Mr. F. Corder says in his recently-published "Modern Musical Composition": "There are two ways of looking at this subject [of variation-writing]. Either the writer wants to stick to his text—to say the same thing over and over again in different language, or else he wants to shew how many absolutely different character-pieces the same raw material can give birth to. The display-variations of the old *virtuosi* exemplify the first view; the Piano-variations of Beethoven and Brahms illustrate the other." Here are two typical instances of the latter method:—

Elaborate variations.

BRAHMS.—Variations on a theme by Handel (Op. 24).

cres.
f
&c.
Part of Variation 24.
p
p
7
f
f
&c.

Of course, where the theme is kept well in view, and the variations are merely decorative and ornamental, the popular mind can understand; and the very ease with which this sort of thing could be followed led to the publication—particularly during the early and mid-Victorian era—of shoals of vapid, threadbare, and atrociously inartistic sets of variations on operatic airs, etc., which were nothing more than a string of platitudes consisting of showy arpeggios, shakes, or groups of repeated notes, whose poverty only served to disguise the even greater poverty of the theme itself. These effusions were, it must be confessed, the delight of our rather immediate ancestors, and school-room pianos rang with the strains of "Warblings at Dawn," "Silvery Waves," "Maidens' Prayers," *et hoc genus omne!*

Inartistic variations.

Such things are now, happily, not only dead, but beyond the power of resurrection, and it almost goes without saying that between these and the Variations of the great masters there is a "great gulf fixed." Variation writing at its best affords and, it is safe to predict, will continue to afford composers many an opportunity for the display of some of their highest powers, particularly that of developing and bringing out the possibilities of a germ-idea—one of the surest signs of strength and mastery.

Our musical illustrations have already included three or four examples of the kind of movement with which composers usually follow their slow movement. On pages 33 and 36 were shewn instances of the use in this connexion of the Minuet, and (on page 45) of the Scherzo, its more modern successor. As the reader will doubtless remember, the Minuet or Scherzo is usually followed by a Trio (which forms the "Theme of contrast"), at the conclusion of which it is played over again in its entirety. The form of each of these little movements is, in the majority of cases, the simple Three-part or Ternary form, with which we are already familiar.

The *Finale* of a Sonata or Symphony, which is nearly always a quick movement, may take the shape of a first movement as regards its form, with Exposition, Development and Recapitulation, or it may be cast as a Rondo. In isolated cases other designs are met with, such as a Theme with Variations (as in Beethoven's Piano Sonatas in E (Op. 109) and C minor (Op. 111), and his "Eroica" Symphony); a Fugue (as in the same master's Piano Sonatas, Op. 106 and 110); or a slow movement (as in Tschaïkowski's "Pathetic" Symphony).

The Finale of a Sonata or Symphony.

The Rondo: its two varieties.

As we have already discussed the First-movement form and the Theme and Variations, it will be necessary now merely to make a passing allusion to the *Rondo*. Two varieties of Rondo are in existence, called the Older (or Simple) Rondo, and the Modern (or Sonata-) Rondo. The former of these is one of the most primitive of musical types, and may be expressed by the following formula :—

$$A—B—A^2—C—A^3 \text{ etc.}$$

where A represents a short principal theme, recurring from time to time after sections of contrast, or Episodes (B, C, etc.). Of such a Rondo, the "Arabeske" of Schumann (Op. 18) is a well-known instance; but, for simplicity from the listener's point of view, the Finale of Haydn's Piano Sonata in D (No. 7) can hardly be surpassed. It sets out with a merry little theme, beginning thus :—

A Rondo by Haydn.

This comes to a definite cadence, and is followed at once by the first Episode, in the tonic minor key :—

This is also complete in itself. The principal theme then comes back again, and after it appears the second Episode, in G major :—

A short passage of transition connects this with the final return of the principal theme, which is presented in full, as before, two "*ff*" chords serving as a finish, or Coda, to the whole.

The obvious squareness of the Older Rondo form, with its various themes all "self-contained," and—so to speak—leading nowhere in particular, has caused composers to modify the form in the direction of greater continuity, and the result is that a more elaborate kind of Rondo has in most Sonatas taken its place. In this the first Episode *recurs at a later period of the movement*, and so becomes practically as important as the Second Subject of a First-movement. The themes themselves, too, are not cut off from one another and separated into "water-tight compartments," as in the Older Rondo; but lead

The Modern Rondo.

more connectedly one into the other. The design may be made clear thus:—

A—B—A^2—C—A^3—B^2—A^4—Coda.

Here A represents the Principal Subject, B the Second Subject (recurring as B^2), C an Episode or theme of contrast, *occurring only once.* Of such a Rondo there are several excellent examples in the Sonatas of Beethoven. One of the clearest of these is that in the Sonata in E flat (Op. 7), the outline scheme of which is as follows:—

A Modern Rondo by Beethoven.

A. Principal Subject (from commencement of movement to bar 16):*

Transition to Second Subject (bar 16 to bar 36).

B. Second Subject (bar 36 to bar 48):

Link, or transitional bars (bars 48–50).

A^2. Return of Principal Subject (shortened)—(bar 50 to bar 62).

C. Episode, or Theme of contrast (bar 64 to bar 88):

Link, or transitional bars (bars 88–93).

A^3. Return of Principal Subject (varied)—(bar 93 to bar 109).

Transition to Second Subject (bar 109 to bar 129).

B^2. Return of Second Subject (transposed into tonic)—(bar 129 to bar 141).

Link, or transitional bars (bars 141–142).

A^4. Return of Principal Subject (varied and shortened)—(bar 142 to bar 154).

Coda (founded upon the Principal Subject, and afterwards reminiscent of the Episode (bar 155 to end).

* The numbering of the bars is reckoned from the first *complete* bar of the movement.

Here our consideration of the form of the Sonata or Symphony must end, and we must refer the reader for more detailed information on the subject to any standard work on Musical Form.* It is hoped, however, that by a perusal of the foregoing pages he may be assisted in his listening, and be enabled consciously to follow—at any rate, to some extent — the unfolding of the composer's plan. If such be the case, he will have taken a great step forward, for the grasping of the general outline or shape of a composition is a powerful aid towards its comprehension, and in a very marked way helps us to escape from that haze of mere sensuous impressions, which, in the case of far too many persons, represents the beginning and the end of their listening to music.

Perception of form a great help in listening.

CHAPTER IX.

THE VARIOUS PERIODS OF MUSICAL COMPOSITION.
I. FROM BACH TO BEETHOVEN.

For the purpose of the average concert-goer, the art of instrumental music rarely goes further back than the period of Handel and Bach. From time to time examples of work anterior to that period may be heard—harpsichord music, it may be, by such men as Purcell, Couperin, and Domenico Scarlatti; but of the compositions of these earlier instrumental writers—important as they are—it is unfortunately impossible to speak here in detail, owing to exigencies of space. Our aim in the chapters that follow must be very briefly and simply to indicate, so far as can be indicated by verbal description, some of the chief characteristics of the music of those whom we may regard as the outstanding figures of the last two hundred years.

So far, then, as instrumental music is concerned, the "line of succession" is more or less as follows :—

Periods of modern music.

(i) The period of Bach and Handel.
(ii) The period of Haydn and Mozart.
(iii) The period of Beethoven and Schubert.
(iv) The period of Mendelssohn, Schumann and Chopin.
(v) The period of Wagner, Brahms, Tschaïkowski, Dvořák, César Franck, and Grieg.

---

* The matter is fully set forth in the present writer's "Form in Music.' (Joseph Williams, Limited.)

(vi) The period of Strauss, Debussy, Elgar and others of the modern school.

Certain distinguished names are omitted from the above list, simply because the bulk of their work was achieved outside the realms of purely instrumental art—and for the present it is upon this aspect of music only that we intend to speak.

Importance of German music.

One thing that strikes the observer in considering this line of succession is that, until comparatively recent years, the battle has been fought out almost exclusively on German or Austrian soil. The great contrapuntists, Bach and Handel, were German; in or near the Austrian capital were "hammered out" by Haydn and Mozart the principles of the great musical forms, the Sonata and the Symphony; in Vienna also Beethoven's and Schubert's most important work was done. Then, a little later, the Romantic movement in music had its representatives in Schumann and (in a much lesser degree) in Mendelssohn, both of German birth and education. Contemporary with these last-named composers, however, comes François Frédéric Chopin, in whose music the language of Romance spoke with a different voice. By birth a Pole, his life-long residence in Paris imbued him with much of the French spirit, and by the blending of the national characteristics of both France and Poland there was produced a quite unique style, peculiarly Chopin's own, which has neither been imitated with success, nor founded a so-called "school."

Poland.

Russia, Bohemia and Norway.

Coming to more recent times, the art of instrumental composition has found exponents of note in Peter Ilitsch Tschaïkowski the Russian, Antonin Dvořák the Bohemian, and Edvard Grieg, the Norwegian. The French school includes a writer of much significance in the person of César Franck,* who in turn has been followed by the no less remarkable Claude Debussy. Germany, meanwhile, since the time of Brahms, after passing through a short period not of inactivity, but of comparative mediocrity, is again to the fore with Richard Strauss, while among other names of note may be included those of Alexander Scriabin and Igor Stravinsky (Russia), Maurice Ravel, Paul Dukas, and Florent Schmitt (France), A. C. Mackenzie, C. V. Stanford, Edward Elgar, Frederick Delius, Vaughan Williams and Gustav Holst (Great Britain), Jan Sibelius (Finland), etc.

France and England.

It will now be our object to point out a few of the leading features of each of the above-named periods; in the case of the first period—that of Bach (1685-1750) and Handel (1685-1759)—

* César Franck was actually a native of Liège, in Belgium, but lived nearly all his life in France.

we must realize that the music will in the main be more or less *contrapuntal* in its nature; that is to say, it will usually present itself to our minds in the form of two or more separate melodies running side by side, to each or all of which we must, in varying measure, give attention. This is frequently called Polyphonic (*i.e.*, many-voiced) music, and is well illustrated by the succeeding extracts:—

Contrapuntal writing of Bach and Handel.

HANDEL.—"Allemande" from Suite in G minor (No. 16).

&c.

BACH.—"Caprice" from Partita in C minor.

*** The different parts, or "voices," in this example are written on separate staves, for the sake of clearness.

Then, again, we may often find a whole movement based upon one kind of melodic outline, perhaps little more than the persistent carrying-out of one form of "figuration" based upon some such scheme as the following :—

BACH.—Prelude in D from the 48 Preludes and Fugues.

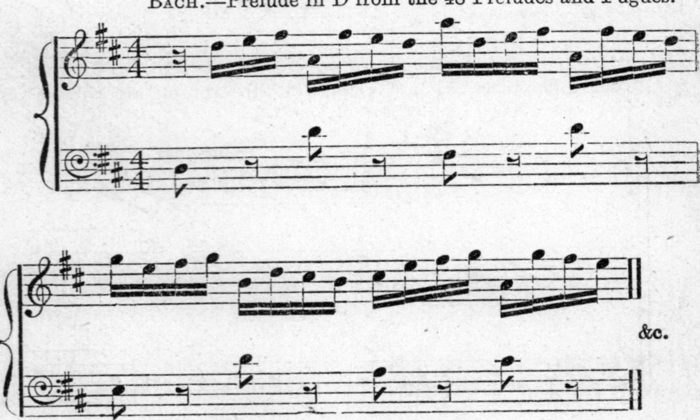

The idea of providing contrasts of thought *within the movement itself*, by playing-off one theme against another of different character had—in these days—yet to be arrived at, and so it is that, in the instrumental pieces of the Bach-Handel period, the music so often flows on and on in a continuous stream, unbroken and unmarked by those points of arrest or contrast which we look for in the writings of later men.

Internal contrast yet to be achieved.

With Bach especially, however, the interesting nature of his figures, and his perfection of detail, over and over again blind us to the lack of diversity of subject-matter; at times he is so *modern* in his harmonies, so rich in the texture of his ideas, that it is difficult to imagine that his music was written about two hundred years ago. Indeed, whereas the music of his contemporaries—even much of that of Handel—sounds to present-day ears more and more old-fashioned and archaic, that of Bach seems constantly to yield up surprises in the shape of unexpected and hitherto unrealized beauties of thought and expression, causing us to feel that, even if he writes in the idiom of a bygone age, the spirit revealed in his music is perennially fresh and young.

Modern character of Bach's harmony.

Comparing the styles of Bach and Handel, we shall notice that, whereas Handel's harmonies are generally peculiarly simple, straightforward and diatonic, those of Bach are richer, more subtle, and of a far more chromatic nature—indeed often astonishingly so. Witness the difference in the harmonic character of a "Sarabande" from each composer:—

The styles of Bach and Handel compared.

HANDEL.—"Sarabande" from Suite in G minor (No. 16).

Andante.

&c.

BACH.—"Sarabande" from English Suite in G minor.

The Haydn and Mozart period.

The period of Haydn (1732–1809) and Mozart (1756–1791) is remarkable for the growth of a style of writing in which the melodic interest is concentrated in some one particular part or voice—supported by chords or subordinate figures of accompaniment—instead of being distributed amongst several parts or voices. As so often exemplified in history, the beginnings of new discoveries or inventions—though fraught with untold possibilities of future development—often compare unfavourably with the conditions they will ultimately modify or supplant; and in the history of music we find that this is notably the case. The early attempts at the style of writing alluded to above, when set side by side with the wonderful polyphony of Bach, sound singularly feeble, poor, and meagre; and yet a new door was being opened, and a road indicated along which music was to develop in the future in utterly undreamt-of ways.

The clear-cut rhythm of this period.

One very marked feature of the music of the Haydn-Mozart period is the clear-cut nature of its rhythm; and the evident delight with which composers strung together regular strains of four bars, together with the comparative novelty of their effect, led in many cases to little care being taken over the *quality* of either melody or harmony. Over and over again trivial tunes supported by a poverty-stricken accompaniment were accepted in lieu of the severer counterpoint of the older writers, and, even with Haydn and Mozart themselves, the following kind of thing was sometimes the result:—

Occasional triviality.

But, as we pointed out on page 59, the occurrence of incidents of this kind must not blind us to the magnificent heritage bequeathed to us by these early writers of the Viennese school. As a master of varied rhythms, Haydn even now stands in some ways unrivalled; his themes, with their *naïveté* and their natural flow, sound to-day as fresh as ever, and throughout his best work, as Sir W. H. Hadow says, "the whole sentiment is as pure and sweet as a spring landscape." Listen

Haydn's freshness.

to this theme, with its odd and sportive admixture of phrases of five, seven, and four bars in length:—

HAYDN.—Minuet from String-Quartet (Op. 76, No. 3).

Although to the experienced listener the music of Mozart is full of individual character-touches which distinguish it

Affinity of style between Haydn and Mozart.

from that of his elder contemporary, it is none the less true that, in general style, there is a considerable likeness and affinity between the two. Every period of musical history has its own special idioms, its own peculiarities of language, which are to be found more or less in the work of all composers living during that period; and (over and over again) passages will occur in the works of the two great writers we are considering which it would puzzle the very elect to assign off-hand to their respective sources. Particularly is this the case with the cadences and phrase-terminations, and certain "transitions" similar to those shewn on pages 58 and 59; but, apart from such conventional coincidences, it often happens that in the spirit, if not in the letter, the two masters draw very near together. Witness the following themes—each from a slow-movement of a Symphony:—

HAYDN.—"Adagio" from Symphony in E♭ (No. 3).

Adagio. *pp* *tr* &c.

MOZART.—"Andante" from Symphony in D (No. 5).

Speaking in general terms, it may be said that the music of Mozart, if lacking the humour, the homeliness and the

Some distinctions of style.

raciness of that of Haydn, exceeds it in grace, in elegance, and in an exquisite finish, that are entirely his own and distinguish his writings in a notable degree from those of his contemporaries. A lovely iridescence, too, runs through many of his passages, attained by the use of chromatic harmonies which, while full of tenderness and delicacy, never lapse into sentimentality :—

MOZART.—Symphony in G minor (1st movement).

This G minor Symphony of Mozart has rightly been described as the "supreme achievement of 18th century instrumental music,"

The early works of Beethoven.

and it needed the genius of Beethoven (1770–1827), to carry the art forward into a region hitherto unknown. The early works of this great master follow somewhat closely the spirit

Beethoven's debt to Haydn and Mozart.

and the manner of his immediate predecessors. The first Sonatas and the two Symphonies in C and D major are full of points which shew this; could anything be more Mozartean than this cadence?—

BEETHOVEN.—Symphony No. 1, in C.

or more Haydnesque than the following bustling Coda to the first movement of the Symphony in D?—

BEETHOVEN.—Symphony No. 2, in D.

Early originality.

And such unconscious reflections as these are only natural as illustrations of the generous enthusiasm of a great mind as yet only in the growing stage—immature, it is true, but big with promise. Certain touches, even in his earliest works, are prophetic, such as the wonderful drop of the long G in bars 9–10 of the following extract from his Op. 1, to the unexpected F sharp, and the subsequent entry of the theme in the far-away key of B minor:—

BEETHOVEN.—Trio for Piano and Strings, in C minor (Op. 1, No. 3).

pp
pp
pp
&c.

It is not, however, until somewhere about the year 1804 that we find the real Beethoven. With the "Eroica" symphony he seemed to break for ever with the past, and—to use his own words—"to step along a new road." The distance travelled, as it were, between his earlier productions and this amazing symphony is perhaps unique. Henceforward, in Beethoven's music, we find a "personal note," new in the history of instrumental art. Its existence has an analogy in English literature, which may serve to illustrate this point. If we take the novels of Sir Walter Scott, for instance, we feel and know that he is, throughout, the story-teller pure and simple; we get little or no clue to the nature of the *man* through his writings. With an author like Thackeray, on the other hand, we are admitted on many an occasion into the inner chamber of his being. "Thackeray's novels," says a modern literary critic,* "are one prolonged personal confession." In a different way and under different conditions, we can realize to some extent a similar change when we compare the music of Beethoven with that of his predecessors; here we seem to see a revealing of the man himself in his works, which, to those who know them, is unmistakable.

The "personal note" in Beethoven's music.

It is customary to speak of Beethoven's music as dividing itself into three periods, and although such a classification can only be approximate, it has a certain value in enabling us to understand a little of his mental progress. The *first period*, then, may be said to include the early trios for pianoforte and strings, a few of the first pianoforte sonatas, and the first two symphonies. The *second period* dates, roughly speaking, from the production of the "Eroica" symphony, and includes almost all the remaining pianoforte sonatas—save the last three or four—his pianoforte concertos, the violin concerto, many of the string-quartets, and the symphonies from No. 3 to No. 8. The *third period* embraces the latest string-quartets, the last few pianoforte sonatas, and the great "Choral" symphony. These works of the third period were all written in the isolation of complete deafness; they frequently contain passages which even to modern ears sound obscure and crabbed, and which are certainly difficult to understand. On the other hand, it is here that his themes reach at times a depth and an intimacy of expression which has never been surpassed. If we think for instance of such movements as the following, we shall get a glimpse

Beethoven's three periods.

The last works.

* W. J. Dawson—"Makers of English Fiction."

of the spirit that was moving through these extraordinary compositions :—

BEETHOVEN.—P. F. Sonata in B♭ (Op. 106).

or, later in the same movement :—

Ibid.

Beethoven's power of development.

We have already seen, in our analysis of Beethoven's Sonata in G (Op. 14, No. 2), a little of the master's constructive skill, his power of musical development. It is in this marvellous ability to take full advantage of the possibilities of his themes that he stands supreme, and is the despair of many a modern musician. We append one more example—part of the Coda in the last movement of the Symphony in F. Let the reader observe the extraordinary rhythmic diversity, and the way in which the interest is thus kept alive:—

Later in CODA.

Strings.

f

(c)

Wind instruments.

f

'Cellos & Basses.

*** In this last extract it should be noticed that the rhythmic figure of the main theme is now in crotchets instead of quavers, and that the melody in minims in example (*b*) is now given out "forte" both descending and ascending, being treated at the 5th bar in shorter notes than at first, thus imparting a wonderfully increased sense of impetus, which is maintained until the music reaches a climax some few bars later.

Lastly, Beethoven's music—though inevitably more complex than that of his predecessors, through his endeavour to express deeper things—shews us the perfect balance of the elements of melody, harmony, and rhythm. "In his hands the forces of design and of expression were completely controlled. Self-dependent instrumental art on the grandest and broadest lines found its first perfect revelation in his hands, not in a formal sense alone, but as the highest phase of true and noble characteristic expression."*

CHAPTER X.

THE VARIOUS PERIODS OF MUSICAL COMPOSITION. II. FROM SCHUBERT ONWARDS.

Schubert: his productivity.

CONTEMPORARY with Beethoven, we meet with a remarkable figure in Franz Schubert (1797-1828). The catalogue of Schubert's compositions reaches the extraordinary total of eleven hundred and thirty-one works, including apparently ten symphonies, twenty string quartets, twenty-four pianoforte sonatas, eighteen dramatic works, eight masses and other choral pieces, and no less than about six hundred songs! When we consider that all this astounding activity was compressed into the short space of thirty-one years of life, we hold our breath in sheer amazement. At the same time, the reflection as to the singularly small proportion of these works that remains in general acceptance to-day forces itself upon us, and compels us to try to discover at any rate a few of the causes for the clear neglect of so much that poured from his brain in such marvellous profusion. First and foremost must be placed the facts of an imperfect education musically (he was almost entirely self-taught); and—consequent upon this—an inability effectively to criticize his own work. Schubert therefore never gained what may be termed artistic self-control; he simply poured forth that astonishing wealth of ideas in song, symphony, sonata, or what not, without stopping seriously to consider whether those ideas were in their right setting—whether they were focussed aright, so that they might produce their intended effect. In other words, he is perhaps the most striking example of the partial failure of the untutored genius, the man whose inspiration is not guided, restrained, strengthened by the experience that comes from passing through the school of discipline.

Schubert's weakness.

---

* Sir H. Parry.

Of Schubert's instrumental works, the early ones shew the impress of Mozart, of whom he was a fervent admirer; but when we reach his later compositions, we are conscious of something that is entirely new and personal. There is a touch of romance and fancy about them that is purely a product of his own imagination; and we feel, moreover, that he is in a very special sense a "colourist." He creates an atmosphere, and seems to revel in the sheer loveliness of each chord he writes, each orchestral shading he paints in.

The Romantic element in Schubert.

A modern writer has the following :—" When Keats tells of

'Magic casements, opening on the foam
Of perilous seas in faery lands forlorn,'

it is not the picture alone which gives us delight: *each word* has a charm, a colour: the exquisite thought is crowned with a halo not less exquisite. And much of Schubert's melody is in the very spirit of Keats. The themes of the Unfinished Symphony, of the first pianoforte trio, of the octet, are the incarnation and embodiment of pure charm; every note, every harmony, every poise of curve and cadence makes it own appeal and arouses its own response."*

It is thus that Schubert excels; in design, in the placing his thoughts in that design so that they shall "tell" in the best possible manner, he is far inferior to any of his great predecessors; but as a colourist he is unique. And by this we do not mean exclusively an orchestral colourist; we mean a colourist in his melody, his harmony, and especially his modulations—as in this wonderful passage :—

Schubert a colourist.

SCHUBERT.—" Andante " of the Unfinished Symphony.

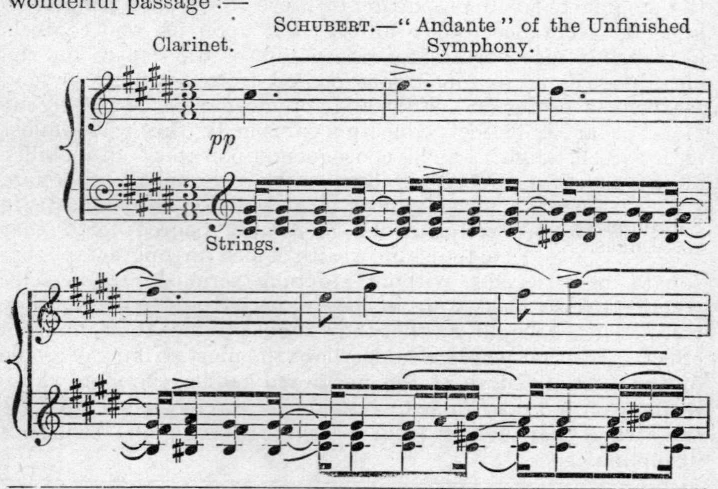

* Sir W. H. Hadow—" Oxford History of Music."

With Schubert came the dawn of the Romantic movement in music. "Romantic music," says the late Mr. Dannreuther in the "Oxford History of Music," "is, in some sense, an offshoot of literature, a reflex of poetry . . . . a desire to produce musical effects suggested by natural phenomena." It came later in point of time than did the Romantic movement in literature, but it had its roots in the same source, namely, a keen love of the past and its traditions and legends, with their witchery and their poetic appeal. "Everywhere," says Mr. Dannreuther again, "there were musical echoes of nature, recollections of 'unhappy, far-off

The Romantic movement in music.

things,' appeals to sentiment and emotion which would lose half their force had they not been anticipated by literature."

This Romantic element in music reveals itself to some extent in the work of Mendelssohn (1809–1847); but more fully in that of Schumann (1810–1856) and Chopin (1810–1849). One sees it in the tendency to associate music with some idea or ideas *outside itself*. For instance, it is on record that Mendelssohn, when travelling in Scotland, sent a letter home to his parents from Fingal's Cave, with the following theme at the head of it:—

to shew, as he said, "how extraordinarily the place affected me." This theme he later on expanded into the beautiful overture known as "Die Hebriden," or "Fingal's Cave," which, to the listener with any imagination, seems to breathe the very spirit of "the land of the mountain and flood." This touch of pictorial suggestiveness is to be found in his "Italian" and "Scotch" Symphonies, and even in his wonderful boyish overture to Shakespeare's "Midsummer Night's Dream," which—as Sir George Grove used to say—"brought the fairies into the orchestra and fixed them there":—

Mendelssohn's picturesqueness.

MENDELSSOHN.—Overture to "A Midsummer Night's Dream."

It is this faëry-like spirit which animates Mendelssohn's Scherzos, and makes them in their own special way unique. At the time of their composition these Scherzos introduced an entirely new element into the range of musical expression, equally remote from the geniality of the Haydn and Mozart Minuets and the grim humour of the Beethoven Scherzos. They are in fact more akin in spirit to certain incidents in the work of Carl Maria von Weber who, in his opera of "Oberon" and elsewhere, was the first writer to lead us musically into Elfland. Mendelssohn, too, had a remarkable facility in the invention of flowing, graceful, often expressive—but rarely soul-stirring—tunes; he is seldom at a loss here, and the reader will doubtless recall the manner of the composer in such a passage as the following, typical of many others:—

The faëry-like element.

Typical Mendelssohnian manner.

MENDELSSOHN.—Piano Concerto in D minor.

Occasionally—as in his beautiful violin concerto—this gift of spontaneous tune is seen in a peculiarly attractive guise; on the other hand, it degenerates at times into something perilously near the sentimental, as in one or two of the "Lieder ohne Worte"—charmingly graceful and fresh as most of them are—and in parts of the pianoforte concertos. Then, too, it must be confessed that Mendelssohn was somewhat of a mannerist: certain stereotyped progressions of melody or harmony, especially at the endings of phrases, occur too frequently for us not to feel that this is the case, *e.g.*:—

Conventional types of phrase.

However, when all is said and done, we have to recognize that Mendelssohn enriched the art of music in practically every department, and in all of these his transparent "cleanliness" of style and his perfect mastery over all the resources at his command compel our admiration and afford us delight. He never bungles; he knows what he wants, and also knows how to get it; where some men—notably his contemporary, Robert Schumann—fail, even though possessed with ideas in themselves greater, Mendelssohn succeeds through sheer *savoir faire;* and, if he does not stir us to the depths, his power to charm is undeniable, and irresistible to those with whom such things as purity of thought and perfection of setting are qualities which count.

Mendelssohn's great qualities.

To Schumann and to Chopin the Romantic movement in music appealed with singular force in different ways. Schumann, the romantic of the romantics, steeped from his early years in the poetry of Jean Paul Richter, and seeking to portray in music ideas hitherto expressed only in the language of words; Chopin, the adored of Parisian *salons*, blending

Schumann's Romanticism.

the idioms of his native Poland with the elegance of his French training;—both form an interesting and attractive topic upon which to enlarge. We must, however, merely indicate two or three features in their music which may serve as some sort of guide to the listener and prepare him for what to expect, when he meets their work. First, then, in Schumann we have to deal with a man who, in his poetic zeal, was inclined at times to chafe under the requirements and necessities of musical construction. In his anxiety for the direct expression of his ideas, he often failed to realize how much that expression depended for its effect upon the way in which such ideas were set forth. Consequently, we find that his work not unfrequently falls short of its full meaning and intention, simply through the weakness of its form. In his smaller pieces this weakness often shews itself in its rhythm; the phrases proceed in an almost unvarying succession of four-bar groups, and the music has a habit of "halting" periodically, which is fatal to continuity. The first of the "Davidsbündler" (Op. 6) is a striking example of this. After an introduction of five bars, the main theme commences thus:—

Schumann's weakness in design.

SCHUMANN.—"Davidsbündler" (Op. 6).

closing in G major, the tonic key, at the eighth bar. Henceforward the music runs on in a practically continuous series of four- and eight-bar periods, every period ending in the same way with a perfect cadence in G major.

And yet, how beautiful, how truly the poet he is, times without number! Who can resist the spell of the opening subject of the pianoforte concerto, with its exquisite touch of yearning, its note of sadness:—

Poetic nature of his themes.

SCHUMANN.—Pianoforte Concerto in A minor.

Allegro affettuoso.

&c.

or remain cold to the fire and animation of the "Finale" of the C major Symphony?* Then, too, what a wealth of imagination is revealed in the slow-movement of the same symphony, the three "Romanzen" (Op. 28), the little piece entitled "Vogel als Prophet," and the "Phantasiestücke" (Op. 12), the first of which, "Des Abends," begins as follows, with its fascinating blending of duple and triple times:—

SCHUMANN.—"Phantasiestücke" (Op. 12, No. 1).

* The opening of this is quoted on page 134.

Such things are among the priceless possessions of our musical heritage, and will live secure in our affections so long as human nature is susceptible to beauty of thought and expression.

Although some of the music of Chopin may here and there lay itself open to the charge of a certain "luxurious effeminacy," the majority of it is so unique in the language it speaks, and it is so full of tenderness, of grace, and of passion, that we recognize in it the hand of a supreme master in his own sphere. That sphere was a limited one, it is true; Chopin wrote for the pianoforte only, his one or two excursions into the realm of orchestral and vocal art were complete failures, and he himself knew that his strength lay in the treatment of the instrument of his choice. When dealing with it, he is entirely original; his effects are absolutely his own, his idiom personal to himself: think of the essentially Chopinesque ornamentation, with its "shimmer" and its gossamer delicacy —an ornamentation which is not *merely* embellishment, but part of the very life of the themes themselves:—

The character of Chopin's music.

Originality of his pianoforte writing.

or take note of the no less individual character of his melodic figures and of his harmonies :—

and it will not be difficult to see something of the direction in which Chopin influenced the art of pianoforte-writing, even if he did little of moment in other departments of composition. There is nothing heroic in Chopin, and for the constructive or "architectural" side of music—the planning of works on a large and important scale—he had little or no aptitude. He was content to express himself in the simplest musical designs, and did so with an attractiveness and a charm which rarely fail.

Wagner: his influence on later composers.

Of Richard Wagner (1813–1883) it may safely be said that, by his commanding genius, he has exerted more influence over the art of music than any other writer of modern times. All have come under his sway, and a comparison of the works written since his period of activity with those prior to that date will reveal a striking difference of expression, not only in degree, but in kind.

Advance in art of writing for the orchestra.

The dramatic element in music, so wonderfully manifested in "Tristan und Isolde," "Die Meistersinger," "Der Ring des Nibelungen" and "Parsifal," has found its way into purely orchestral composition in a manner utterly unknown before, largely owing to the great advance in the art of scoring for the orchestra which has been one of the most striking results of Wagner's work. He it was who first made the orchestra to "glow" with that marvellous wealth of colour, and imparted to it that power of emotional effect which had only been partially realized by his predecessors. Added to this mastery over the orchestral force we find, particularly in his later productions, a richness and luxuriance of harmony and a truly astounding polyphony (*i.e.*, interweaving of melodies), producing an intensity of expression which, in its own special way, has no parallel. Witness the poignant opening harmonies of "Tristan":—

Wagner's harmony and polyphony.

or the unutterable sadness and despair of the modification of this theme when Tristan lies wounded to the death in the third act of the drama:—

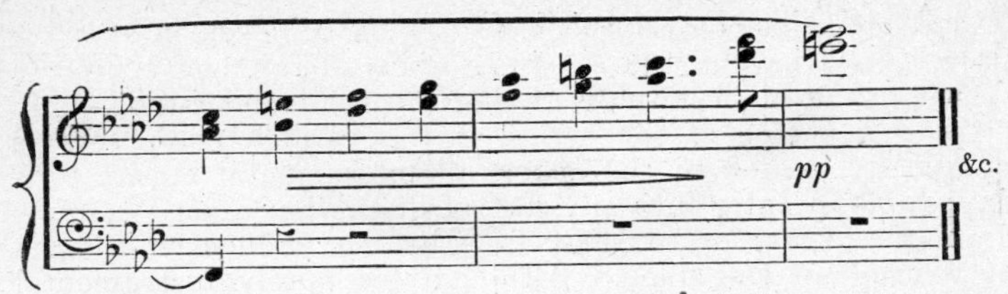

Think, too, of the wonderful epitome of the whole opera of the "Meistersinger" given to us in that amazingly brilliant prelude—in which geniality and humour reign supreme—and note how freely Wagner moves in contrapuntal fetters! Here are three themes combined with the ease that only comes of supreme mastery over technical means :—

Wagner's ease in combining themes.

Con moto. WAGNER.—"Die Meistersinger."

1.

2.

3.

&c.

Such things belong to the category of achievements which have passed beyond the region of criticism, and have become classic in the highest sense of that much misunderstood word.

As this sketch of the styles of the various composers is practically limited to the sphere of instrumental music, it is impossible to enter into any sort of discussion upon Wagner's dramatic ideals, or to shew how he has influenced the art of writing for the stage. Although his purely instrumental works are few in number, they are of the highest significance, and any review of the musical art which should leave his doings out of account would manifestly be absurdly inadequate, considering how every composer since his time—whether writing for the stage or not—has come under his sway and has been affected, consciously or unconsciously, by his genius.

Mannerisms.

That the mannerisms of Wagner—and, especially in his early works, he had undoubted mannerisms—should have been seized upon and worked to death by the "weaker brethren" amongst modern composers was only to be expected, and this has served to bring such things into somewhat high relief, of which the inevitable Wagnerian "turn" is one example among many :—

The true student of musical history, however, will put such matters in their proper place, and realize that they count for little when considered side by side with the marvellous enrichment of the range of musical expression which is due to the work of this extraordinary man.

Brahms.

The next notable name we meet with is that of Johannes Brahms (1833–1897). It cannot be said that the precise position that is the due of his music is a matter which has passed altogether out of the region of dispute. Men are still divided into two more or less hostile camps, the one containing those who see in Brahms the direct successor of Beethoven, with a large share of that master's spirit; the other containing those who see in him only the somewhat austere and even uninspired composer, who perchance may appeal to the intellect, but who does not reach the heart.

Opinions upon his work.

A distinguished musician on one occasion said to the present writer, "I don't know of any great composer who has written so little really beautiful music." Another critic has said, "That Brahms stands beside Bach and Beethoven is hardly any more a matter of controversy . . . . All three are . . . . artists, in whose supreme mastery of utterance the highest message has found fit and adequate expression."

And so the battle is waged.

Characteristics.

Brahms' work is nearly always lofty in conception and contains a wealth of idea that is remarkable; his grasp of the "architecture" of his music is firm and sure. Strength and dignity are nearly always characteristic features of his writing, but it must be confessed that the guise in which he puts forward his thoughts is not always the most attractive or winning, so that his music sometimes fails in sheer beauty of sound—a result largely due to the frequent thickness of his harmonies and his orchestration.

Of humour or of fairy-like delicacy of touch Brahms shews little trace, and the fact that he rarely writes a Scherzo seems to point out that he himself felt that he had not the qualities that make for success in this particular direction. He has a peculiar fondness for themes formed upon the notes of the common chord—often with one note omitted, thus :—

BRAHMS.—Symphony in C minor (No. 1).

and delights in a rich and expressive sonority of harmony and in overlapping rhythms and cross-accents such as the following :—

BRAHMS.—"Intermezzo" (Op. 118).

At times, too, his subjects are singularly "Beethovenish" in manner and feeling:—

BRAHMS.—Symphony (No. 2) in D.

Surely the spirit of the Bonn master was not far from his successor when this theme was written!

Compare the opening of the "Eroica" Symphony:—

BEETHOVEN.—Symphony (No. 3) in E flat.

In Antonin Dvořák (1841–1904) we meet with a musician who in a very special sense may be described as *national.*

Dvořák: a national composer.

Born in a little village in Bohemia, his early life was passed entirely amongst the "people," and from the bands of wandering players and singers who came from time to time to his native village from Prague or Pressnitz, he absorbed a wealth of Bohemian national tune which sank into his very being, and prepared the soil for the production of those peculiarly individual compositions which later on came from his pen in rich profusion. As a result of this, we find that his music exhibits in a notable way the qualities of rhythmic life and glowing colour. He is always at his best when he allows himself thus to reproduce the characteristic melodies and rhythms of his native land, and in such moments he carries us away with the *entrain* of his style. Think of

Characteristic rhythms.

the opening of the first of his Slavische Tänze, with its cross-accents and its wayward alternations between the keys of G minor and G major :—

and many equally felicitous passages in others of these dances, and some little clue will be afforded as to his happy utilization of this national element.

How exquisitely expressive he can be melodically can be gathered from the opening of the lovely melody which forms the principal subject of the "Largo" of his "New World" Symphony :—

Tschaïkowski.

The Russian spirit.

When we turn to Peter Ilitsch Tschaïkowski (1840–1893), we find another distinctly national composer. Just as the music of Dvořák is typically Bohemian in spirit, so that of Tschaïkowski is essentially Russian in its idiom. This is shewn both in the underlying sadness of many of its themes as, for example, the opening of the E minor symphony:—

and again in the almost barbaric nature of its rhythm and its colouring, as in the Finale of his pianoforte concerto:—

Tschaïkowski's skill in orchestration and the occasional weakness of his themes.

Tschaïkowski delights in the powerful, sensuous effects of sound obtainable from the modern orchestra, for which he writes with consummate skill and mastery, even if at times he lays the colour on somewhat too thickly, as in the noisy "1812" Overture. Indeed, it must be confessed that this mastery over the resources of orchestral effect hides up now and then the somewhat undistinguished and even trivial character of certain of his themes. Even the well-known opening subject of the "Pathetic" Symphony is hardly free from a suspicion of the common-place:—

TSCHAÏKOWSKI.—Symphony in B minor (No. 6).

although its subsequent development in large measure atones for this. The late Edward MacDowell, the American composer, put the matter very neatly when he said—in comparing the music of Tschaïkowski with that of Brahms—"Tschaïkowski's music always sounds better than it is; that of Brahms is often better than it sounds." From the foregoing remarks, it will readily be understood that Tschaïkowski is at his best in his orchestral music; in chamber-music, where the possibilities of mere colour are less, he is not quite so much at home, and some of his weakest work is to be found in his pieces for the pianoforte alone.

Present-day Writers

The work of such men as Richard Strauss (1864–), Claude Debussy (1862–1918), Edward Elgar (1857–1934), and other writers of the more modern school, cannot be discussed at length in the present small volume. Nothing is more noteworthy, however, than the very divergent styles of the two first-named writers. Strauss, the apostle of a bold realism, with his thunderous orchestra and his often daring polyphony:—

RICHARD STRAUSS.—"Domestic Symphony."

Debussy, the dreamer and the "impressionist," painting with subdued tints and making a purely sensuous appeal to the listener—the two men represent the opposite poles of modern art, and are in a sense typical of the trend of German and French thought respectively.

Strauss and "thematic development."

Debussy's harmonic scheme.

Technically, Strauss carries the process of "thematic development" to extraordinary lengths, and his themes undergo transformations and are combined in a manner which—whether it carries conviction or not—certainly denotes acquirements of a very high order; Debussy, on the other hand, may be said often to dispense with definite melodic themes altogether, and makes his effects largely from successions of shifting harmonies, of a certain elusive charm and fascination :—

CLAUDE DEBUSSY.—"Sarabande" for Pianoforte.

The "Tonal" scale.

In the process, he frequently employs a special form of scale, consisting of a succession of whole tones, thus :—

which, even granting its effectiveness in certain situations such as the following :—

CLAUDE DEBUSSY.—"L'Après-midi d'un faune."

soon outwears its welcome and palls upon the ear by reason of its inevitable monotony. It is clear that where a scale presents no variation in the size and quality of its intervals from degree to degree, the possibilities of contrasted character between these various degrees are reduced to a minimum, and even the harmonies built upon such a scale are of limited scope, and take on the same monotonous colouring. Thus we must be prepared, in the work of Debussy and some others of the extreme modern French school, for mannerisms such as the following, which it must be confessed, appear over and over again *usque ad nauseam* :—

CLAUDE DEBUSSY.—String Quartet in G minor.

In conclusion, we hope that, imperfect and incomplete as such a brief survey of the various periods in the history of modern music must of necessity be, some little help may have been afforded to the listener who wishes to put himself in an attitude for intelligent appreciation of the special characteristics of the writers who may be regarded as representative and typical of the growth of the art during the last two centuries or more. The reader may pursue the subject further in "The Art of Music" (Hubert Parry), "Studies in Modern Music" (W. H. Hadow), "The Growth of Music" (H. C. Colles), the present writer's "Cameos of Musical History," and in other works mentioned on pages 155 and 156.

CHAPTER XI.

THE STORY OF THE SYMPHONY.

In the preceding chapters of this volume frequent reference has been made to the Symphony; but, beyond stating that, in form, it is practically identical with the Sonata—that it is, in fact, a Sonata for the orchestra—we have said little about its development as a branch of the composer's art. We purpose, therefore, in the present chapter, to give a rapid sketch of the principal points of interest in its history, so that those who listen to symphonies in the concert-room may do so with some little idea of the special characteristics attaching to this important class of composition at various stages in its career.

It would seem that the term Symphony began first to be seriously employed much in the same way as the word Sonata, and, as was pointed out on page 54, both terms were then indifferently applied to those works, or to those portions of works, where the music was to be *played*, and not sung. We find the word Symphony first used to signify the "ritornelli," or instrumental introductions or interludes, that occurred from time to time during the course of the operas written at the beginning of the 17th century. Such a symphony (so-called) is to be found in one of the very earliest operas, Peri's "Euridice," written and performed in Florence in 1600. It is scored for three flutes, and has a certain amount of character of its own. Here it is:—

Early uses of the term Symphony.

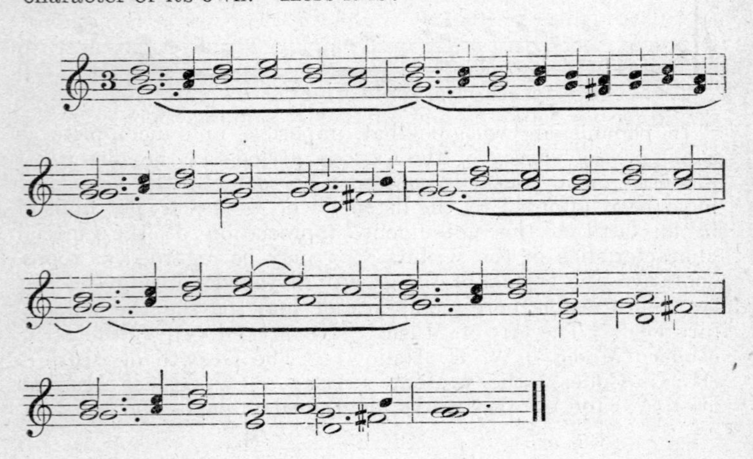

This application of the term Symphony lived on for a considerable time, and we must now try to see how the word became limited in its meaning to something more akin to its modern use. The introductions and interludes of which we have spoken were still, it is true, called symphonies; but, after a while, longer instrumental pieces began to find a place in the operas of the period, and the first of these pieces, that which preceded the opera, became the special recipient of the title. The composer clearly had more scope here than elsewhere in the opera for writing a successful instrumental piece, as he was not restricted as to length, or time taken in performance, as would be the case during the progress of

Narrowing-down of the meaning of the word.

the action. These first "Symphonies" were, of course, very crude; instrumental music as an art separate from vocal music was only in its cradle, so to speak; and men had to set themselves the task of finding out the form or design most suitable for such things—no small labour, where practically nothing existed upon which to base their operations! So, for some time, little more was attempted beyond getting a sort of rough balance of effect, a contrast of "fast" and "slow," such as might give a certain feeling of variety—then, as now, a factor of the greatest importance.

Crudity of the earliest examples of Symphony-writing.

From these early experiments issued (i) The French Overture and (ii) The Italian Overture. Here again, the title Overture must not be confused with the modern composition of that name; terms were loosely used at the period we are considering, and often the words Symphony, Overture, Concerto, etc., were employed indiscriminately to represent works of identical, or almost identical, pattern.

The French Overture and the Italian Overture.

These two forms, the French Overture and the Italian Overture, were akin to one another in having their origin in the desire for that element of variety and contrast to which reference has been made; they differed in the way in which that variety was obtained. The French Overture, dating from the time of Jean Baptiste Lulli (1633–1687), was in three movements, viz. a broad, slow movement to begin with, followed by a quicker one (often fugal in character), and concluding with a slower piece, generally in the shape of a stately dance, such as the Minuet.

Lulli.

This type of work was extensively employed, and as late as the time of Handel it still maintained its ground, Handel himself adopting it for—amongst others—the overtures to "Samson" and "Judas Maccabæus." The overture to the oratorio of "Messiah" has the slow first movement followed by a fugue, and it is said that there is in existence a Minuet which had been originally intended to form the third part. Possibly, however, Handel felt the incongruity of such a piece in a work whose subject was so sublime and sacred as that of "Messiah," and the Minuet does not appear in the score of the oratorio.

The historical importance of the other type of overture, the "Italian," is far greater than that of the "French." It consisted similarly of three movements; but these were in the order of *quick, slow, quick*, an arrangement which composers found more fruitful of effect than that which obtained in the "French" model. Alessandro Scarlatti (1659–1725) had an important share in the establishing of the Italian overture, and by the middle of the 18th century it seems to have

A. Scarlatti.

become quite familiar, and extremely popular. Operas by Hasse, Leonardo da Vinci, Piccini, Jomelli, Sacchini and Galuppi, all have this form of overture; but it is to be feared that theatre audiences then were no more attentive to what preceded the rising of the curtain than they are to-day! Burney, in the account of one of his tours for the purpose of gathering materials for his Musical History, says:—

Reminiscences by Burney, the historian.

"The music at the theatres in Italy seems but an excuse for people to assemble together, their attention being chiefly placed on play and conversation, even during the performance of a serious opera." Apparently card-tables were put out during the performance, and the "quality" would attend when a singer of the "first class" was on the stage, or when some particular situation seized their fancy. For the rest, the music troubled them but little, least of all the overture; so that composers had not much inducement to put forth their best work into the "Sinfonia avanti l'Opera," or symphony before the opera. Hence it came to pass that the better of these symphonies, or overtures, were played apart from the operas, and gradually we find them assuming a separate existence, listened to for their own sake, and judged accordingly. Henceforward, composers were impelled towards a higher standard of writing, and thus the foundations of the modern symphony were laid. In this constructive work Alessandro Scarlatti, to whom allusion

Form of early symphonies.

has already been made, was much to the fore. His opera overtures (or symphonies, as they were often called) were usually in the three short movements of the Italian manner (Allegro, Adagio, Allegro). Occasionally, an Adagio would precede the first Allegro, in the style of an Introduction, a feature which has been perpetuated in many of the symphonies of a later date.

Scoring.

Scarlatti's little symphonies were scored with a certain amount of skill for stringed-instruments, to which occasionally he added trumpets and a few other wind instruments. These merely strengthened the strings in full passages, but of scoring in the modern use of the term there was none; the feeling for orchestral colour had not been as yet developed; but by degrees this, as well as a surer method of dealing with the internal form of the movements themselves, became apparent, and the art of symphony-writing grew rapidly in interest and value.

Although Haydn has—in some senses rightly—been called the "father" of the modern symphony, we must remember

Predecessors of Haydn.

that there were certain other men during his period, who were doing good "spade-work" in the development of the symphonic form. Amongst such men were Karl Friedrich Abel (1725–1787),

Johann Christian Bach* (1735–1782)—son of the great Johann Sebastian—and Georg Christoph Wagenseil (1717–1779). Karl Stamitz (1746–1802), another writer of symphonies, is also worthy of remembrance as the conductor of the renowned Mannheim Orchestra, then regarded as the first in Europe.

The Mannheim Orchestra.

Burney says of this orchestra: "It was here that the *crescendo* and *diminuendo* had birth, and the *piano* (which was before chiefly used as an echo) . . . . as well as the *forte* were found to be musical colours, which had their shades as much as red and blue in painting." He then adds:—"I found, however, an imperfection in this band, common to all others I have ever heard . . . . the defect I mean is the want of truth in the wind instruments. I know it is natural to these instruments to be out of tune, (!) but some of that art and diligence, which the great performers have manifested in vanquishing difficulties of other kinds, would surely be well employed in correcting this leaven which so much sours and corrupts all harmony. This was too plainly the case to-night with the bassoons and hautboys, which were rather too sharp at the beginning, and continued growing sharper to the end of the opera!"

Position of the symphony at the time of Haydn.

By the time of Haydn the following points in symphony-writing had been more or less clearly established:—

(i) The three-movement form of the symphony was practically universal —a fourth movement (as in a symphony in D by Stamitz) being occasionally inserted.

(ii) The old purely contrapuntal style of writing had given way to a great extent to a more *harmonic* style, (in which the melody of a single part often became supported by a subordinate accompaniment), and the value of effects of harmony as a means of expression was beginning to be realized.

(iii) The idea of contrasting one theme or subject with another in the course of the same movement was pretty definitely recognized as a valuable element in the production of interest and variety.

---

* "Mr. J. C. Bach seems to me to have been the first composer who observed the laws of contrast, *as a principle*. Before his time, contrast there frequently was in the works of others; but it seems to have been accidental. Bach in his symphonies and other instrumental pieces, as well as his songs, seldom failed, after a rapid and noisy passage, to introduce one that was slow and soothing. His symphonies, of which the harmony, mixture of wind-instruments, and general richness and variety of accompaniment are certainly the most prominent features, seem infinitely more original than either his songs or harpsichord pieces."—Burney—"History of Music."

(iv) Instrumental execution had greatly improved, and composers were beginning to have some little idea as to the grouping of instruments for the purposes of colour.

Haydn's work.

With the art at this stage in its development, came Haydn upon the scene, to perfect the *form* of the symphony, and to infuse into it that wonderfully living spirit which so much of his work exhibits. In his hands, it took the shape which has been the basis of the operations of all succeeding symphonic writers.

Patronage of the artist.

At this period of the world's history—the middle and latter part of the 18th century—the only way in which the artists and musicians of the day could hope to succeed, or even obtain a livelihood, was to attach themselves — much as literary men did in England—to wealthy patrons, who, in return for board, lodging, uniform, and the wages of a fairly good cook, expected them to conduct their private bands, and to provide them with agreeable musical accompaniments to their dinners. At times, of course, the patron—often a Prince, Archduke or Archbishop—may have been a true amateur of music: in such a case, the lot of the music-director, or "Kapellmeister," was more congenial, if not more lucrative. Haydn held a succession of such posts, his salaries ranging from about £20 to about £78 per annum! However, during this period he composed innumerable symphonies and other works, in which he gradually advanced in the scope and expressiveness of his ideas, and in the richness and variety of his orchestration.

The Kapellmeister.

Character of Haydn's work.

Haydn nearly always adopted the *four*-movement plan for his symphonies, introducing as the third of these the Minuet and Trio, a class of piece into which—as we saw in Chapter IV—he infused a degree of geniality, kindliness and fun, which are peculiarly his own. In one very notable direction, too, Haydn put new life and meaning into the symphonic structure. The son of a peasant of Croatia, he had from his earliest years become imbued with a love of the national folk-songs, which became veritably part of himself. Here, in association with these "people's tunes," he got into contact with something natural and true—as distinct from the artificiality and affected mannerisms of the polite world of the day, and throughout his writings the freshness of the rhythms and the naïve simplicity of the themes are, directly or indirectly, due to the influence upon Haydn of these national melodies—the veritable expression of the sentiment of the people living in closest communion with Nature.

Peasant-tunes.

Freshness and variety of Haydn's rhythms.

It is interesting to note that the opening melody of the Symphony in D (No. 4), written in 1794, is said to be actually a native dance of the South Slav peasantry, entitled a *Kolo*. Here is the first phrase, a quaint one, in five-bar rhythm :—

Mozart, like Haydn, held two or three posts during his life as musical director of the private bands of certain wealthy patrons, one of these being the Archbishop of Salzburg. The experience of orchestral effect which he gained from the holding of these positions compensated him, let us hope, in some small degree for the galling position, socially, in which he found himself. With the Archbishop of Salzburg, particularly, he seems to have been on the worst of terms, for we find him writing to his father as follows :—" The two valets in attendance, the controller, the court-quartermaster, the confectioners, two cooks, and my '*littleness* ' (a delightful expression of sarcastic contrast to his "*Highness*"—his master) " dine together. The two valets sit at the head of the table, and I have the honour to be placed just above the cooks."

Mozart.

The indignity of Mozart's position as Kapell-meister.

Mozart's first symphony of real historic value and importance is the one entitled, " The Parisian," in D major. It was composed in 1778 (at the age of twenty-two) for one of the " Concerts Spirituels " in Paris—(hence its name). It appears that the orchestra at these concerts rather plumed itself on its *attack*, and Mozart was given to understand beforehand that, if he wished to please everyone, and make a success, he must take great pains to give the band plenty of opportunity to

Mozart's first noted symphony.

exhibit their prowess in this direction. He was further to remember that the Parisians would stand nothing that was not short, bright and sparkling; for depth or elaboration they cared not a jot! Mozart took these hints, and we find him beginning the symphony with this passage:—

The "Parisian" symphony.

MOZART.—Symphony in D (No. 9).

Here was scope for "attack" at the very outset! Everyone was pleased; the band had got what they wanted, and the audience burst into applause at the "crashing" opening passage. Mozart, in a letter, amusingly describes how he anticipated, when writing the work, the places at which "the audience would clap their hands"! This symphony is in three movements, and is one of the most fully-scored of all his works in this department, consisting as it does of flutes, oboes, bassoons, horns, trumpets and drums, in addition to the strings.

Score of the work.

During the next ten years Mozart completed all that he was destined to do in the department of symphony, and throughout this period we find how much the subjects gain in character and meaning, how their development becomes more amply worked out, how the various instruments of the orchestra gradually play a more independent and important part in the scheme of colour—in fact, how the whole plan seems to be conceived upon a broader basis and with a loftier aim.

Mozart's advance in symphony-writing.

Mozart had one great advantage over Haydn in having travelled more, and having by this means been able to hear the orchestras of Munich, Paris, and Mannheim, while Haydn, until quite late in his life, was practically limited to his own. From the Mannheim band Mozart learnt much, and doubtless the result of this experience is shewn in many a passage of beautiful orchestral colouring. Indeed, it is hardly possible to estimate with sufficient appreciation the debt of gratitude we owe to Mozart (and indeed, to Haydn also, in his later works) for the development of the individual tones of the orchestra. From the time of the "Parisian" symphony onwards almost every instrument has something distinctive to say, and the modern art of orchestration may thus be said to have had its birth.

Mozart's scoring for the orchestra.

In the preceding chapter we referred to the extraordinary leap forward made by Beethoven in the "Eroica" Symphony, and we have alluded to the *personal* element in the more mature of his works. The upheaval in social conditions at the time of the French Revolution was making itself felt in music as in everything else, and many of the newer political and social ideas had a ready sympathizer in Beethoven. It was inevitable that his strong, rugged independence of character should—sooner or later—come into conflict with the polished, brilliant hollowness of the society into which he found himself cast. And come into conflict it did in an unmistakable way, both personally and through his music.

Beethoven.

The "Eroica," one of the very longest symphonies on record, produced—as might have been expected—amazement and even hostility on the part of audiences accustomed merely to be amused. The depth and earnestness of the work and the consequent demands it made upon the intelligence of the hearers were, to say the least, baffling to a public hitherto unprepared for such seriousness of aim, and contemporary criticisms contain many opinions like the following:—"Although there is no lack of striking and beautiful passages in which the force and talent of the author are obvious, the work seems often to lose itself in utter confusion"! At the Conservatorium at Prague, too, it was "held in horror as *dangerously immoral*"!

The "Eroica" Symphony.

Contemporary criticisms.

Now, however, the "Immortal Nine"—as Beethoven's Symphonies are often called—have passed beyond the region of such criticism, and are secure in the affections of musicians, who see in them the highest manifestation of the classic spirit in music. It is impossible to comment at any length upon these symphonies, and the reader is referred for many interesting details respecting their history, and for an analysis of their form, to Sir George Grove's "Beethoven and his Nine Symphonies," which in many senses constitutes a valuable

The "Immortal Nine."

commentary for the amateur. The following table may prove useful:—

Symphony No. 1	C major	Produced in 1800
" " 2	D "	" 1803
" " 3	E♭ major (*Eroica*)	" 1805
" " 4	B♭ major . . .	" 1807
" " 5	C minor	" 1808
" " 6	F major (*Pastoral*)	" 1808
" " 7	A major	" 1813
" " 8	F "	" 1814
" " 9	D minor (*Choral*) .	" 1824

The "Choral" Symphony.

It will be noticed that the Ninth Symphony has the title of "Choral." This is in reference to the fact that in its final movement—a setting of Schiller's "Ode to Joy"—a chorus and a quartet of solo voices are added to the usual orchestral force—a proceeding which was then without precedent, and which (if we except the Symphony-Cantata of Mendelssohn, the "Hymn of Praise") has never been followed since by any composer of the first rank.

The Symphonies of Beethoven in many senses unsurpassed.

Beethoven, then, advanced the art of symphony-writing to a point beyond which, up to the present, it has seemed hardly able to go. Looking back, and comparing the colossal grandeur of the "Choral," with the earliest little symphonies of Haydn and Mozart, it is amazing to note in how short a space of time this extraordinary advance has been made. As Felix von Weingartner, the eminent German conductor, writing in 1899, said: "It was only about the year 1760 that Haydn wrote his first symphonies, and in 1823, these harmless and playfully serene productions had been developed into the most sublime of tragedies; Beethoven had written his Ninth Symphony. More than seventy-five years have passed since the appearance of that wonderful work, and in the realm of symphony it still wears the crown without dispute."

The work of less typical men.

Just as the history of a nation is in a very real sense the history of its greatest men, so the record of an art may be said to be that of its most distinguished exponents; it does not, however, follow from this that the "lesser lights" of any particular period contribute nothing to the common stock, or that their own achievements are valueless. On the contrary; we have already seen how, in the middle of the 18th century, such men as Abel, Johann Christian Bach and others were instrumental in paving the way for Haydn and Mozart. Unequal to the highest demands upon the artist, they yet did good work and acted as pioneers in a movement that was then beginning to assume great importance, namely, the definite recognition of the harmonic, as distinguished from the purely contrapuntal, side of music. Other men, too, of inferior but by no means despicable talent, were writing and producing symphonies during the period of Haydn and Mozart, to the admiration of the audiences of the time. Among such were François Joseph Gossec, Andreas and Bernhard Romberg, Carl Dittersdorf, and others, some of whom were then regarded as the rivals and even the equals of Haydn and Mozart.

Schubert.

When we come to the time of Beethoven, we find considerable activity on this side of musical art; but there is one name that stands out in strong relief amongst those of his contemporaries—that of Franz Schubert. As we pointed out in Chapter X, Schubert's genius lay rather in the region of emotional expression than in that of construction; consequently we find much of his most abiding work in the smaller musical forms notably in his songs. However, he wrote several symphonies, of which only that in C major, beginning thus:—

and the two movements constituting the "Unfinished," in B minor, are permanent items in present day programmes.

The great Symphony in C major.

The Symphony in C major, beautiful as are its ideas, strongly as the genius of its composer asserts itself again and again, suffers, as the late Sir G. A. Macfarren used to say, from its great *lengthiness*—as distinguished from mere *length*. Whole passages are repeated without variation, the themes, instead of being developed, are merely re-stated, and—exquisite as are the thoughts contained in the work—the effect of the whole is not unlike that of some precious stone or gem badly set, shorn of its full attractiveness by imperfect workmanship.

The "Unfinished" Symphony.

On the other hand, the "Unfinished" Symphony always seems to the present writer as nearly perfect a thing as can well be imagined. Even its form—Schubert's weak point—is excellent, and as for its tunes, who ever penned a more lovely one than the Second Subject of the first movement?—

Spohr.

Of Ludwig Spohr (1784–1859) as a symphonic writer, we may say that his art, although refined and often poetical, was too redolent of his own peculiar and persistent mannerisms, and too lacking in virility and in nobility of thought, to exercise any very great influence, or make any permanent mark in the evolution of the symphony. His best-known work in this department is that known as "Die Weihe der Töne," or "The Power of Sound," which is illustrative of a poem by a writer named Pfeiffer. It is consequently an example of what we know as "programme-music," by which is meant a musical work intended to portray certain ideas, in themselves independent of music—just as Beethoven's "Pastoral Symphony" was intended to reproduce in our minds some of the feelings aroused by the contemplation of the country and country-life. Spohr also wrote what he called a "Historic" Symphony, in which the four movements are supposed to represent four distinct musical periods. The first is that of Handel and Bach; the second, that of Haydn and Mozart; the third, of Beethoven; and the last, of what Spohr himself calls the "quite newest" period—namely, that exemplified by himself!

The "Italian" and "Scotch" Symphonies of Mendelssohn.

In Mendelssohn's two most important symphonies, the "Italian" and the "Scotch," we are conscious again of an attempt to relate the music to certain ideas outside itself, and to create a special "atmosphere" by its means. In the latter of these this is particularly the case, the Scherzo producing a "local colour" by including certain melodic and rhythmic features peculiar to Scottish tune; witness its opening theme with the "snap" at the end of the phrase:—

The spirit at work in the whole symphony may be gathered from Mendelssohn's having written the first sixteen bars in the Chapel of Holyrood Palace—as he himself says, "open to the sky and surrounded with grass and ivy and everything ruined and decayed." This is how the work begins:—

"Mendelssohn had great readiness for making a tune, and it is as clear as possible that when he went about to make a large instrumental work, his first thought was to find a good tune to begin upon." This assertion of Sir Hubert Parry is well evidenced by the opening subjects of the two symphonies already referred to, the "Italian" and the "Scotch":—

Tune-like character of Mendelssohn's subjects.

Everyone will admit that these are good tunes, but even the best tune will not of itself make a strong or stirring symphony; for its principal subjects the mind needs something terser, more instinct with nervous force, than can possibly be supplied by the regular periods of a tune, however beautiful. Of course, these remarks apply mainly to the more important movements of a Sonata or a Symphony; in the slow-movement, where the lyrical element prevails, the continuous melody "of linkèd sweetness long drawn out" is eminently in place, and makes a corresponding effect.

In comparing the value of Schumann's contributions to symphonic art with that of Mendelssohn's, we have to realize that in Schumann we have a man who in some respects—notably in the vigour and loftiness of his ideas—comes nearer to Beethoven than do others of that master's more immediate successors.

Mendelssohn and Schumann compared.

In striking contrast with the themes just quoted are the following:—

Striking rhythmic nature of Schumann's themes.

SCHUMANN.—Symphony No. 2, in C major.

How full of energy and rhythmic life they are, how rich in promise for development. And yet it is here that Schumann so often disappoints us, and, instead of the themes "germinating" as with Beethoven, so that we are continually made to feel their fruitfulness, Schumann is often driven—as was Schubert—to the mere *repetition* of his figures, a repetition which soon wearies, simply because nothing grows out of it. His orchestration, too, at times beautiful, is too often uncertain and uninteresting, and in this respect he cannot compare with the more polished, the more masterly, but less poetically-gifted, Mendelssohn. If he had possessed the "technique" of his friend, how great he would have been!

Where Schumann fails.

The four symphonies of Brahms, in C minor, D major, F major and E minor, are undoubtedly the most important symphonic works since Schumann, and, perhaps, since Beethoven. They are strong in the strength that comes from a complete "masterhood," and are conceived on a scale and in a manner which stamps them as works of real moment in the history of symphonic writing.

Brahms.

In marked contrast with the severity of Brahms stands the emotionalism, the fiery energy, of Tschaïkowski, in whose three best-known symphonies in F minor, E minor and B minor ("Pathetic") is to be seen an extraordinary power ot expression, combined with a command of rhythmic life and of orchestral colour that is quite admirable. Qualities such as these have appealed with irresistible force to present-day audiences, and it is quite possible that Tschaïkowski has been placed for the time upon a pedestal he may not be destined always to occupy. However that may be, his work is striking enough to put him in the

Tschaïkowski.

front rank of modern symphonists. His music, like that of Antonin Dvořák is—as we have already seen—full of a national spirit; both men went to the "people's tunes" for their inspiration. In both a strong rhythmic element is noticeable, piquant and picturesque, and over and over again the themes in their symphonies—dissimilar as they are—are based upon the characteristics of native songs and dances,* which impart to them a singular life and freshness. By reason of this their music—whatever else it is—is rarely *dull*.

Dvořák.

National characteristics.

In the later years of the 19th century and the earlier years of the 20th, many composers (notably Richard Strauss), turned their attention from the symphony to the symphonic poem, in which many of the elements of symphonic writing are present, but whose form is determined by some "poetic basis"—possibly a legend or story which the music is intended to illustrate. In the more recent success, however, of Sir Edward Elgar's two symphonies may possibly be seen the beginnings of a reaction against purely "illustrative" music, and of a desire that music shall once more exist independently of a connexion with literature or the other arts. Indeed, the time seems ripe for some notable writer again to shew that, after all, the true function of music is rather that of the creation of a *mood* than of the expression of specific ideas which—when not absolutely untranslatable in terms of sound—are often better expressed by other means.

From this rapid sketch of the rise and progress of the symphony, it will have been seen how its history has been one long unfolding of the possibilities both of design and expression. Little did the writers of those loosely-planned pieces that were played, to inattentive audiences, before the operas of the day in the 17th century, imagine to what a pinnacle of greatness the symphony would attain in the hands of a Beethoven; little did they dream of the loveliness of a Schubert "Unfinished," or of the exhilaration of a Dvořák "New World"; and yet all that has been achieved in the direction of making the symphony the highest form of instrumental art yet conceived has been accomplished in the short space of a couple of hundred years. What the next development will be one cannot tell; the future is "in the lap of the gods," and it will be the task of others to appraise at their true worth the efforts of those, who, in the time to come, will contribute their share towards the advancement of the art of instrumental music and the widening of its power of expression.

Rapidity of the advance of the Symphonic art.

---

* Many of the themes in Dvořák's beautiful Symphony, "From the New World" are based upon the peculiar idioms of negro melodies.

CHAPTER XII.

THE INSTRUMENTS OF THE ORCHESTRA.

The importance of realizing the tone-qualities of orchestral instruments.

THE ability to know and recognize, even in some small degree, the tones of the various instruments in modern use is so vital to the intelligent appreciation of music, that it has seemed advisable to devote a chapter to a consideration of some of the characteristics of such instruments, and to indicate a few means by which the listener may identify their special tone-colours. It is clear that no verbal description of an instrument can convey an idea of its character; this must be arrived at in the only possible way, namely, by *hearing* it. All that can be done, therefore, is to give illustrations of the several "voices" of the orchestra, and to quote a few typical extracts from works which the reader is likely to be familiar with—or with which it is easy for him to become familiar. By this means, it will be a comparatively simple task for him to connect in his mind the tone-character of some one or more of such passages with the special instrument by which it is played; and by so doing, he will have some sort of standard of tone in his mind to which he can relate other passages concerning which he may be in doubt in his listening.

Before passing on to a brief study of the component parts of the orchestra, it will be well that it should be clearly understood that the various stringed- and wind-instruments are used in two quite distinct ways by composers, according as the music for which they are required comes under the heading either of (i) Chamber Music, or (ii) Orchestral Music.

Distinction between Chamber music and Orchestral music.

The difference between these two departments of composition lies in the fact that in the former, each and every instrument employed is a *solo* instrument; whereas, in the latter, many of these instruments (particularly those of the "string" family) may be duplicated to almost any extent. "For example, one of Haydn's or Beethoven's quartets for first and second violins, viola and violoncello, would always be executed by four *single* players; on the other hand, each of the string-parts of one of these masters' symphonies—though similarly grouped—would be rendered in actual performance by *several* players.

Strings.

In a large orchestra there are often as many as fourteen or sixteen first violins, an almost equal number of second violins, eight violas, and eight or ten violoncellos, with nearly as many double-basses as a foundation to the whole."* The wind-instruments in an orchestra are seldom duplicated in this way, but are used mostly in pairs—a "first" and a "second" of each kind, the number being often increased to *four* in the case of horns, and generally to *three* in the case of trombones. Each wind-instrument player is, therefore, practically a soloist, and the main reason why the wind-parts are not duplicated as are the string-parts is that, in almost every instance, a certain coarseness of tone would result, a coarseness which is not met with when one part is played by several stringed-instruments in unison.

Wind-instruments.

In concerted Chamber-music, the most usual combinations are—(i) The String-Quartet (two violins, viola and violoncello).

Chamber-music—usual combinations.

(ii) The Duet for pianoforte and violin, or pianoforte and violoncello.

(iii) The Trio for pianoforte, violin and violoncello.

(iv) The Quartet for pianoforte, violin, viola and violoncello.

Other groupings are of course to be met with, such as Quintets and Sextets—for strings alone, or in conjunction with the piano—and occasionally one or more solo wind-instruments are employed; the above list, however, represents the combinations that are the basis of by far the greatest number of compositions likely to be encountered by the reader in his attendance at Chamber concerts.

We have already given an extract from the score of a Trio for pianoforte, violin and violoncello, on pages 95–96; our next example will therefore be taken from a String-Quartet:—

* "Form in Music."—Stewart Macpherson.

p

The instruments of the modern orchestra group themselves into four main classes, or "tone-families," as follows :—

The departments of the modern Orchestra.

(i) Strings.
(ii) Wood-wind.
(iii) Brass.
(iv) Percussion.

In the first class are included the Violin, the Viola, the Violoncello and the Double-Bass, and also the Harp (when that instrument is used).

In the second are to be found the Flute, Oboe, Clarinet, and Bassoon, with occasionally the Cor-Anglais (or Tenor Oboe), the Bass Clarinet, and the Double Bassoon.

In the third are comprised the Horn, Trumpet, Trombone, and Tuba; while the fourth class includes the Timpani (or Kettle-Drums) the Side-Drum, the Bass-Drum, the Triangle. Cymbals, and the Glockenspiel (or Bells).

Most amateurs are nowadays familiar with the appearance and the tone of the various stringed-instruments; and, as our space is limited, we shall confine ourselves to giving a few extracts which—together with the pictorial illustrations accompanying them—may help the listener in distinguishing the peculiar tone-qualities of the different members of the "wind" family :—

1. The Wood-wind Instruments.

(The illustrations of the instruments are not drawn to scale.)

(A) *The Flute*—

Examples of its use :—

Tschaïkowski.—Slow-movement of Pianoforte Concerto in B♭ minor Op. 23 (Bars 5–12).

MENDELSSOHN.—"Saltarello" from "Italian Symphony (Bars 6–10).

(ii) Vivacity.

(B) *The Oboe (or Hautboy)*—

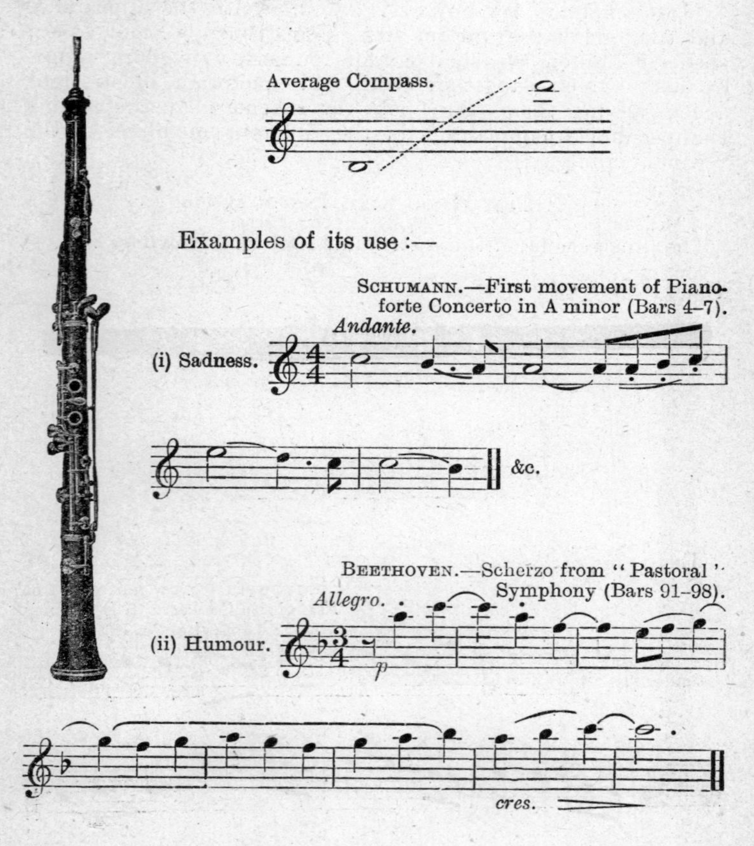

Examples of its use :—

SCHUMANN.—First movement of Pianoforte Concerto in A minor (Bars 4–7).

BEETHOVEN.—Scherzo from "Pastoral" Symphony (Bars 91–98).

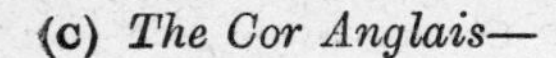

(c) *The Cor Anglais*—

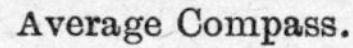

Average Compass.

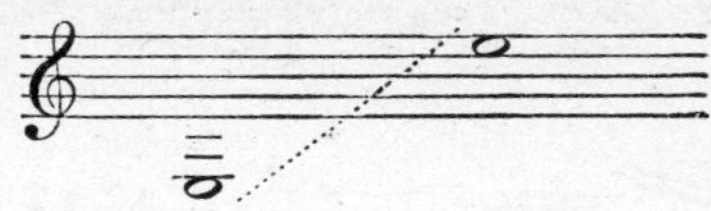

Example of its use:—

DVOŘÁK.—"Largo" from "New World" Symphony (Bars 7–10).

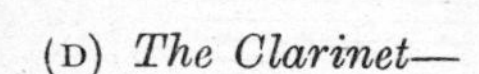

(D) *The Clarinet*—

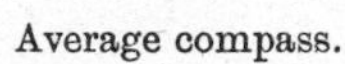

Average compass.

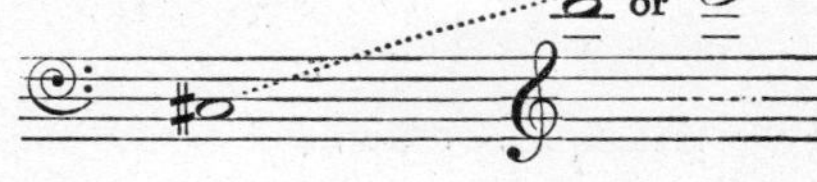

Examples of its use:—

SCHUBERT—"Andante" of "Unfinished Symphony" (Bars 66–83).

MENDELSSOHN.—Scherzo from "Scotch" Symphony (Bars 8–16).

(E) *The Bassoon*—

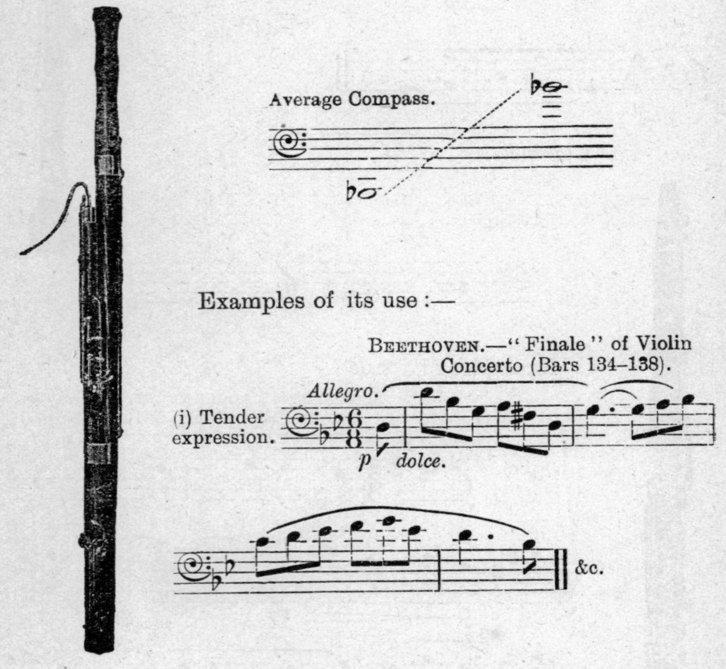

Examples of its use:—

BEETHOVEN.—"Finale" of Violin Concerto (Bars 134–138).

(i) Tender expression.

BEETHOVEN.—Scherzo from "Choral" Symphony (Bars 177–180).

Two Bassoons.

(ii) Humour.

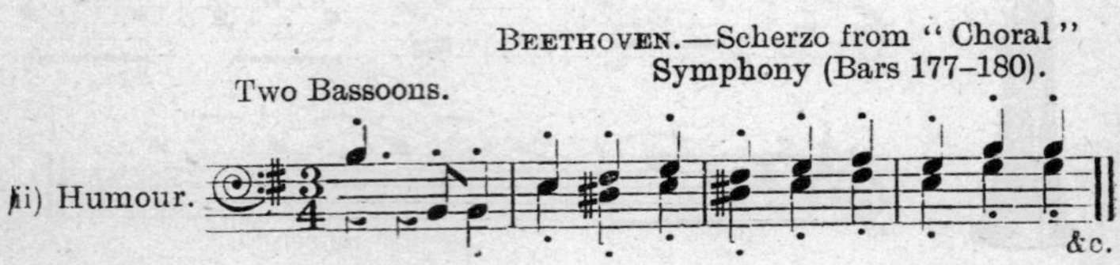

2. The Brass.

(A) *The Horn*—

(B) *The Trumpet*—

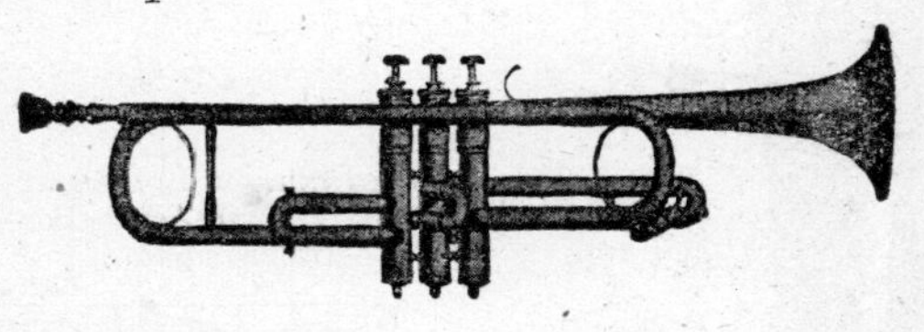

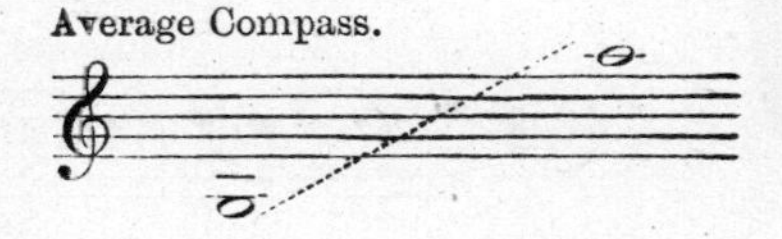

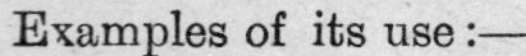

Examples of its use:—

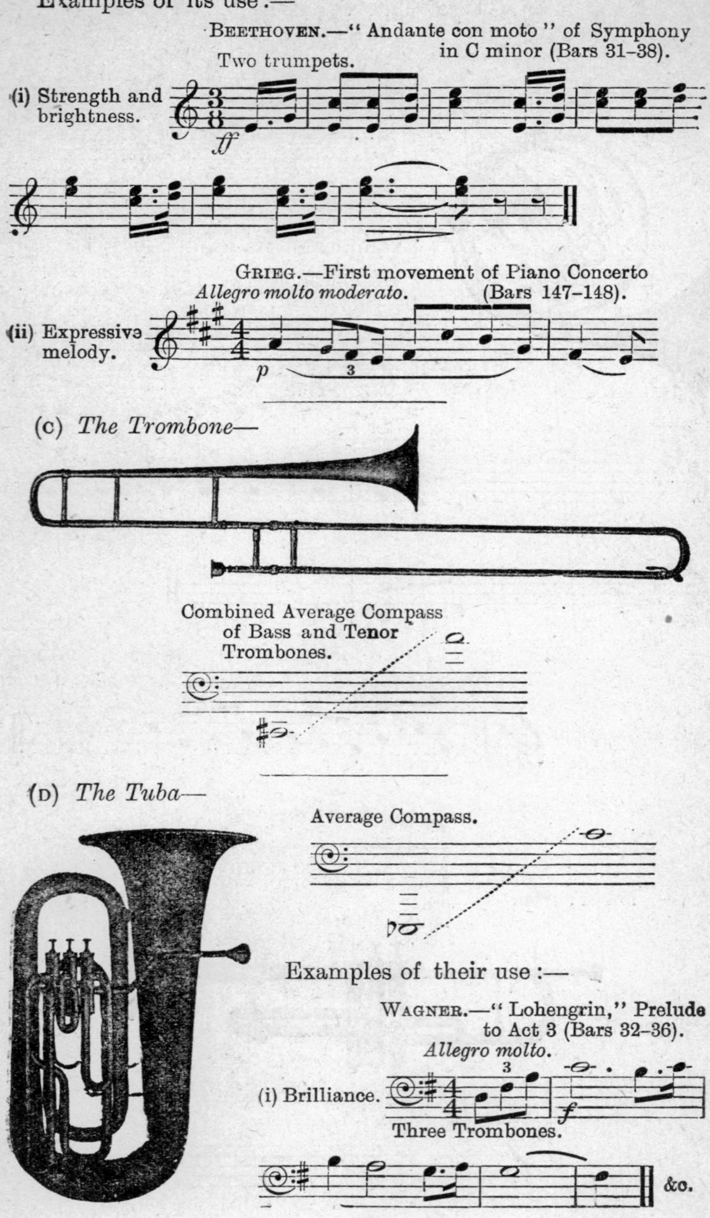

BEETHOVEN.—"Andante con moto" of Symphony in C minor (Bars 31–38).

Two trumpets.

(i) Strength and brightness.

ff

GRIEG.—First movement of Piano Concerto (Bars 147–148).

Allegro molto moderato.

(ii) Expressive melody.

p

(C) *The Trombone*—

Combined Average Compass of Bass and Tenor Trombones.

(D) *The Tuba*—

Average Compass.

Examples of their use:—

WAGNER.—"Lohengrin," Prelude to Act 3 (Bars 32–36).

Allegro molto.

(i) Brilliance.

f

Three Trombones.

&c.

TSCHAÏKOWSKI.—" Pathetic " Symphony (No. 6), commencing
35 bars from end of last movement.

* The Tuba plays the lowest part of the harmony.

---

3. PERCUSSION INSTRUMENTS.

It is needless to give examples of all the various instruments of percussion. Their tones are usually quite unmistakable and—with the exception of the kettle-drums—

The Kettle-Drum—

they are mostly used to produce extra noise, or to add to the vigour and insistence of rhythmical figures. A most effective use of two kettle-drums may however be cited :—

BEETHOVEN.—Violin Concerto (opening of first movement).

Here this characteristic figure of four notes given to the drums is actually the groundwork of much of the first "Allegro" of Beethoven's Violin Concerto, of which the above extract is the opening. The works of Beethoven abound in examples of the masterly use of the kettle-drums; in his hands they first became emancipated from the *rôle* of noise-producing machines, and were exalted to the dignity of a "solo voice" in the orchestra.

Orchestral combinations practically endless.

It goes without saying that the foregoing illustrations and extracts do little more than touch the fringe of the important subject of the modern orchestra. The subtle combinations of the different instruments implied in the expression "scoring for the orchestra," and the endless varieties of tone-colour possible to the experienced composer, cannot here be enlarged upon. Such matters belong to treatises upon orchestration; but if the reader will take the trouble to hear the various works enumerated in this chapter and memorize the effect of the passages quoted—carefully connecting them in his mind with the instruments by which they are played—he will, with a little experience, be able to recognize their tones in such a way that their individuality may be realized, and the enjoyment of listening thereby increased in a notable degree.

Since this volume first saw the light in 1910 the remarkable development of the gramophone has proved a veritable godsend to the listener, by providing him with an ever-present means of familiarizing himself with the changing colours of the orchestral palette. Especially is this the case when the record of any work is followed with score in hand.

A PAGE FROM THE SCORE OF A BEETHOVEN [torn] HONY.*

BEETHOVEN.—First Movement of "Eroica" Symphony (No. 3, in E♭).

* For ease of comprehension in reading, the *actual sounds* produced by the various instruments are given in the above extract. In the composer's score, however, the Clarinets, Horns and Trumpets are written—as is customary—as "transposing" instruments, and thus *appear* to be playing in different keys. These transpositions have reference to the mechanism or fingering of the instruments in question, concerning the notation of which certain traditions have survived.

APPENDIX I.

A LIST OF MUSICAL EXAMPLES ILLUSTRATING THE PRINCIPAL TYPES OF STRUCTURE ALLUDED TO IN PRECEDING CHAPTERS.

THE following extracts have been selected from the works of the best writers as a help to the student, and to the teacher who may wish to enforce his teaching in the best possible way—namely, by a carefully-chosen example. They are typical of countless others of equal value, and may serve as indications of the directions in which such further illustrations may be found. They have in all cases been selected from Pianoforte works, or works of which there are good adaptations for the Pianoforte.

I.—PIECES IN SIMPLE TWO-PART (OR BINARY) FORM.

(*See* "Barbara Allen" quoted on page 20, for this form at its simplest.)

(A) *National Tunes, &c.**

1. "The bailiff's daughter of Islington."
2. "The hunt is up" (2).
3. "The carman's whistle" (4).
4. "You gentlemen of England" (6).
5. "The happy clown" (54).
6. "Come, lasses and lads" (62).
7. "Fairest Isle" (Purcell) (70).
8. "Lady Frances Nevill's delight" (77).
9. "The Bay of Biscay" (79).
10. "Now is the month of maying" (Thomas Morley) (83).

(B) *Instrumental Movements.*

1. "Chaconne" in G major (Theme only) ... ... Handel
2. Minuet in F (No. 6 of "Sept pièces") ... ... Handel
3. Sarabande from 11th Suite... ... ... Handel
4. Allemande from 11th Suite... ... ... Handel
5. Courante from 11th Suite ... ... Handel
6. Courante from 16th Suite ... ... Handel
7. First Lessons in Bach (edited by W. Carroll) Nos. 1, 2, 4, 5, 7, 9, 10, 12, and 15 ... ... Bach
8. Gavotte from "Suite Française" in E ... ... Bach
9. Allemande from "Suite Française" in E ... ... Bach
10. Courante from "Suite Française" in G... ... ... Bach
11. Minuet from "Suite Française" in B minor ... ... Bach
12. Bourrée No. 2 from "Suite Anglaise" in A ... ... Bach
13. Minuet I and Minuet II from Partita in B flat (No. 1) ... Bach
14. Theme of "Andante con variazioni" from Sonata in F, for Pianoforte and Violin (No. 18 in Peters' edition) ... ... Mozart

---

* The numbers in brackets refer to the numbers of the tunes in Hadow's "Songs of the British Islands" (Curwen & Sons).

15. Theme of "Allegretto" (with Variations) from Sonata in E flat, for Pianoforte and Violin (No. 16 in Peters' edition) ... ... Mozart
16. "Andante Cantabile" (as far as 2nd double-bar) from Pianoforte Sonata in C major (No. 2 in Peters' edition) Mozart
17. Six Pastoral Dances (Augener No. 6024a) ... ... Beethoven
18. Theme from Variations upon a March by Dressler ... Beethoven
19. Theme from Variations in Sonata in F minor (Op. 57) ... Beethoven
20. Trio (following Scherzo) in Sonata in A flat (Op. 26) ... Beethoven
21. Minuet (without Trio) in Sonata in E flat (Op. 31, No. 3) Beethoven
22. Trio (following Scherzo) in Sonata in D (Op. 28) ... ... Beethoven

---

II.—Pieces in Simple Three-part (or Ternary) Form.

(*See* "Charlie is my Darling," quoted on page 25, for this form at its simplest.)

(a) *National Tunes, &c.**

1. "The last rose of summer" (5).
2. "The bluebells of Scotland" (12).
3. "Dear harp of my country" (28).
4. "Cadair Idris"—(Welsh melody)—(36).
5. "Song of the Western men" (44).
6. "The Vicar of Bray" (49).
7. "Under the greenwood tree" (57).
8. Minuet, "My Lady's Garland" (89).
9. "Merch Megan"—(Welsh melody)—(91).
10. "The snowy-breasted pearl"—(Irish melody)—(97).

(b) *Instrumental Movements.*

1. "Passepied" in D minor (first part) from 2nd Ordre ... Couperin
2. Minuet in F (No. 7 of "Sept pièces") ... ... Handel
3. First Lessons in Bach (edited by W. Carroll), Nos. 3, 6, 8, and 13 ... ... Bach
4. Minuet (No. 2) from "Suite Française" in D minor ... Bach
5. Menuetto from Symphony in D (No. 4 in Peters' edition) Haydn
6. "Andante" from Sonata in A (No. 26) in Peters' edition) Haydn
7. Minuet in B flat from Sonata in E flat (No. 9 in Peters' edition) ... ... Mozart
8. Minuet in E flat from Sonata in E flat (No. 9 in Peters' edition) ... ... Mozart
9. Minuet in F minor from Sonata (Op. 2, No. 1); also Trio from same ... ... Beethoven
10. Minuet in D major (without Trio) from Sonata in D (Op. 10, No. 3) ... ... Beethoven
11. Menuetto in B flat (without Trio) from Sonata (Op. 22) Beethoven
12. Scherzo in A flat (without Trio) from Sonata (Op. 26) Beethoven
13. "Adagio con espressione" (to bar 24) from Sonata in E flat (Op. 27, No. 1) ... ... Beethoven
14. Scherzo (without Trio) from Sonata in D (Op. 28) ... Beethoven
15. Trio following the Minuet from Sonata in E flat (Op. 31, No. 3) ... ... Beethoven
16. "Lieder ohne Worte" Nos. 1, 7, 13, 19, 20, 22, 27, 28, 30, 31, 37 ... ... Mendelssohn

---

* In many of these tunes, Part I is immediately repeated in order to fit the four-line stanza of words. This does not, however, affect the actual *musical* form which is still that of A—B—A^2.

17. "Erste Verlust," "Wilder Reiter," "Reiterstück," "Nachklänge aus dem Theater," "Erinnerung" (and other pieces in the Album for the Young) ... ... Schumann
18. Davidsbündler (No. 2) ... ... Schumann
19. Mazurkas, Nos. 4, 22, 40 ... ... Chopin
20. "Walzer" (No. 7 of Op. 38) ... ... Grieg
21. "Schmetterling," "Vöglein," "Erotik" "An den Frühling" (Op. 43), and many others ... ... Grieg

---

III.—Instrumental Pieces whose form is based upon that exemplified in the "Minuet and Trio."

(*See* Chapter V, page 42, and Chapter VI.)

1. Any example of a Minuet (or Scherzo) succeeded by a Trio, after which the Minuet (or Scherzo) returns.
2. "Presto" of Sonata in G (No. 10 in Peters' edition) ... Haydn
3. "Andante cantabile" of Sonata in C (No. 2 in Peters' edition)—the whole movement ... ... Mozart
4. Minuets in C, D, and E flat... ... ... Beethoven
5. Allegro in E flat and Trio in E flat minor from Sonata (Op. 7) ... ... Beethoven
6. "Andante" of Sonata in D (Op. 28) ... ... Beethoven
7. Funeral March from Sonata in A flat (Op. 26) ... ... Beethoven
8. "Largo" of Sonata in E flat (Op. 7) ... ... Beethoven
9. Impromptu in A flat (Op. 142, No. 2) ... ... Schubert
10. Third Movement of "Italian Symphony" (Op. 90) ... Mendelssohn
11. "Andante" from Violin Concerto ... ... Mendelssohn
12. "Vogel als Prophet"... ... ... Schumann
13. "Novelletten," Nos. 2, 4 and 7 ... ... Schumann
14. Polonaise in A (Op. 40) ... ... Chopin
15. Impromptus in A flat, G flat, and C sharp minor (Op. 29, 51 and 66) ... ... Chopin
16. Nocturnes in G minor (Op. 37), C minor (Op. 48), and others ... ... Chopin
17. "Albumblätter" (Op. 28, No. 3) ... ... Grieg
18. No. 2 of "Vier Stücke" (Op. 1) ... ... Grieg
19. Slow Movement of "New World" Symphony ... ... Dvořák
20. Klavierstücke (Op. 118, Nos. 2, 3 and 5) ... ... Brahms
21. "Arabesque" in E major (No. 1 of "Deux Arabesques") Debussy

---

IV.—Movements in Sonata Form (or First-movement Form).

It is unnecessary to give a detailed list of first movements in this particular form; any such list would, it is needless to say, be absurdly inadequate, since nearly all the opening movements of Sonatas, Quartets, Symphonies, etc., from the time of Haydn and Mozart to the present day have been written on this plan. We shall, therefore, merely add here a list of pieces (*not* first movements of such works) in this form, which may serve as supplementary examples.

1. "Finale" of Symphony in D major (No. 2 in Peters' edition) ... ... Haydn
2. "Adagio" of Symphony in E flat major (No. 3 in Peters' edition) ... ... Haydn
3. "Andante cantabile" and "Finale" of Symphony in C major (No. 1 in Peters' edition) ... ... Mozart
4. "Andante" and "Finale" of Symphony in G minor, (No. 2 in Peters' edition)... ... ... Mozart
5. "Finale" of Symphony in E flat major (No. 3 in Peters' edition) ... ... Mozart

6. "Andante" of Sonata in F major (No. 1 in Peters' edition) ... ... Mozart
7. "Finale" of Sonata in F major (No. 6 in Peters' edition) Mozart
8. "Andante cantabile" and "Finale" of Symphony No. 1 in C major ... ... Beethoven
9. "Larghetto" of Symphony No. 2 in D major ... ... Beethoven
10. "Finale" of Sonata in C minor (Op. 10, No. 1) ... Beethoven
11. "Adagio con molto espressione" of Sonata in B flat (Op. 22) ... ... Beethoven
12. "Presto agitato" of Sonata in C sharp minor (Op. 27, No. 2) * ... ... Beethoven
13. "Allegretto" of Sonata in D minor (Op. 31, No. 2) ... Beethoven
14. "Scherzo" and "Finale" of Sonata in E flat major (Op. 31, No. 3) ... ... Beethoven
15. "Finale" of Sonata in F minor (Op. 57) ... ... Beethoven
16. "Finale" ("*Le Retour*") of Sonata in E flat major (Op. 81A) ... ... Beethoven
17. "Finale" of Violin Concerto in E minor ... ... Mendelssohn
18. Overture, "Midsummer Night's Dream" ... ... Mendelssohn
19. Overture, "Fingal's Cave"... ... ... Mendelssohn
20. "Finale" of Sonata in E minor ... ... Grieg

V.—Movements in Rondo-Form.

O.R. signifies "*Older-Rondo*" (*see* page 83). M.R. signifies "*Modern-Rondo*" (*see* pages 83-84).

1. "Presto ma non troppo" of Sonata in D (No. 7 in Peters' edition) (O.R.) ... ... Haydn
2. "Adagio" of Sonata in C minor (No. 18 in Peters' edition) (O.R.) ... ... Mozart
3. Rondo in A minor (O.R.) ... ... Mozart
4. "Allegretto grazioso" of Sonata in B flat (No. 4 in Peters' edition) (M.R.) ... ... Mozart
5. "Allegretto" of Sonata in F (No. 1 in Peters' edition) (M.R.) Mozart
6. "Vivace" of Sonata in G major (Op. 79) (O.R.) ... Beethoven
7. "Andante" in F (O.R.) ... ... Beethoven
8. Rondo in C (Op. 51, No. 1) (O.R.)... ... ... Beethoven
9. Rondo in G (Op. 51, No. 2) (M.R.) ... ... Beethoven
10. "Finale" of Sonata in A major (Op. 2, No. 2) (M.R.)... Beethoven
11. "Finale" of Sonata in E flat (Op. 7) (M.R.) ... ... Beethoven
12. "Finale" of Sonata in C minor (Op. 13) (M.R.) ... Beethoven
13. "Finale" of Sonata in E major (Op. 14, No. 1) (M.R.) Beethoven
14. "Finale" of Sonata in B flat (Op. 22) (M.R.) ... ... Beethoven
15. "Finale" of Sonata in D major (Op. 28) (M.R.) ... Beethoven
16. "Finale" of Sonata in C major (Op. 53) (O.R.) ... Beethoven
17. "La consolation" (O.R.) ... ... Dussek
18. Entr'acte in B flat, from "Rosamunde" ... ... Schubert
19. "Moto continuo" from Sonata in C (Op. 24) (O.R.) ... Weber
20. "Arabesque" (Op. 18) (O.R.) ... ... Schumann
21. "Nachtstücke" (Nos. 1, 2, and 3) (O.R.) ... ... Schumann

VI.—Pieces in Variation-Form.

1. "The Carman's Whistle" ... ... William Byrd (1538-1623)
2. "Passacaglia" † from "Suite de pièces" (No. 7) ... Handel
3. Two Chaconnes † in G major ... ... Handel

---

* The *First Movement* of this Sonata is not in Sonata-form.

† These Variations are written upon a *Ground Bass, i.e.*, a Bass which is constantly repeated throughout the Movement.

4. Variations, "The Harmonious Blacksmith," from Suite No. 5 in E major ... ... Handel
5. "Courante avec deux doubles" from "Suite Anglaise" in A major ... ... Bach
6. Variations in F minor .. .. Haydn
7. "Andante" of Symphony in G major (No. 6 in Peters' edition) ... ... Haydn
8. "Andante" of Sonata in D (No. 10 in Peters' edition)... Mozart
9. "Andante grazioso" of Sonata in A (No. 12 in Peters' edition) ... ... Mozart
10. "Andante" of Sonata in G major (Op. 14, No. 2) ... Beethoven
11. "Andante con variazioni" of Sonata in A flat (Op. 26)... Beethoven
12. "Andante con moto" of Sonata in F minor (Op. 57) ... Beethoven
13. "Andante, molto cantabile ed espressivo" of Sonata in E (Op. 109) ... ... Beethoven
14. Six Variations (Op. 34) ... ... Beethoven
15. Twelve Variations on a Russian Theme ... . Beethoven
16. Thirty-two Variations in C minor ... ... Beethoven
17. Thirty-three Variations on a Theme by Diabelli (Op. 120) Beethoven
18. "Variations Sérieuses" (Op. 54) ... ... Mendelssohn
19. "Études Symphoniques" ... ... Schumann
20. Variations in B flat, for two pianos ... ... Schumann
21. Variations and Fugue on a Theme by Handel ... ... Brahms

APPENDIX II.

SOME BOOKS OF REFERENCE CONTAINING FURTHER INFORMATION UPON SUBJECTS DEALT WITH IN THE PRESENT VOLUME.

Ear Training, Rudiments of Music, etc. :—

(i) Frederick Niecks ... ... "Introduction to the Elements of Music." (Augener & Co.)

(ii) Stewart Macpherson ... ... "Rudiments of Music." (Joseph Williams.)

(iii) Stewart Macpherson and Ernest Read "Aural Culture," Parts I, II, & III. (Joseph Williams.)

Harmony, Counterpoint, Fugue, etc. :—

(i) Sir G. A. Macfarren ... ... "Six Lectures on Harmony." (Longmans & Co.)

(ii) E. Prout... ... ... "Harmony: Its Theory and Practice." (Augener & Co.)

(iii) C. H. Kitson ... ... "The Art of Counterpoint." (Oxford University Press.)

(iv) Stewart Macpherson ... ... "Melody and Harmony." (Joseph Williams.)

(v) Stewart Macpherson ... ... "Studies in the Art of Counterpoint" (including Fugue, etc.). (Joseph Williams.)

(vi) James Higgs ... ... "Fugue." (Novello.)

Musical Form :—

(i) H. C. Banister ... ... "Lectures on Musical Analysis." (G. Bell & Sons.)

(ii) W. H. Hadow ... ... "Sonata Form." (Novello.)

(iii) E. Prout... ... ... "Applied Forms." (Augener & Co.)

(iv) Percy Goetschius ... ... "Lessons in Music Form." (Oliver Ditson Co., Boston.)

(v) Stewart Macpherson ... ... "Form in Music." (Joseph Williams.)

History of Music :—

(i) C. H. H. Parry ... ... "The Art of Music." (Kegan Paul.)

(ii) H. C. Colles ... ... "The Growth of Music." (Oxford University Press.)

(iii) "The Oxford History of Music" (7 vols.) ... (Clarendon Press, Oxford.)

(iv) George Dyson ... ... "The Progress of Music." (Oxford University Press.)

(v) Percy A. Scholes ... ... "The Listener's History of Music." (Oxford University Press.)

(vi) Stewart Macpherson ... ... "Cameos of Musical History." (Boosey & Hawkes.)

BIOGRAPHY :—

(i) Sir Hubert Parry ... ... "Studies of Great Composers." (Routledge.)
(ii) Sir Hubert Parry ... ... "Bach." (Putnam & Sons.)
(iii) E. J. Dent ... ... "Handel." (Duckworth.)
(iv) Eric Blom ... ... "Mozart." (Dent.)
(v) Ernest Walker ... ... "Beethoven." (John Lane.)
(vi) Sir George Grove ... ... Articles on Beethoven, Schubert and Mendelssohn in Grove's Dictionary of Music and Musicians. (Macmillan.)
(vii) J. A. Fuller-Maitland ... ... "Robert Schumann." (Sampson, Low & Co.)
(viii) Frederick Niecks ... ... "Chopin as Man and Musician." (2 vols.) (Novello.)
(ix) H. C. Colles ... ... "Brahms." (John Lane.)
(x) Rosa Newmarch ... ... "Tschaïkowski." (John Lane.)

THE ORCHESTRA :—

(i) E. Prout... ... ... "The Orchestra." (2 vols.) (Augener & Co.)
(ii) F. Corder ... ... "The Orchestra, and how to write for it." (Curwen & Sons.)
(iii) Ch. M. Widor ... ... "The Technique of the Modern Orchestra."(Joseph Williams.)

MISCELLANEOUS :—

(i) Sir George Grove ... ... "Beethoven and his Nine Symphonies." (Novello.)
(ii) W. H. Hadow ... ... "Studies in Modern Music." (2 vols.) (Seeley & Co.)
(iii) F. Corder ... ... "Modern Musical Composition." (Curwen & Sons.)
(iv) Frederick Niecks ... ... "Programme Music." (Novello.)
(v) Ernest Newman ... ... "Musical Studies." (John Lane).
(vi) J. S. Shedlock ... ... "The Pianoforte Sonata." (Methuen.)
(vii) Robert Schumann ... ... "Music and Musicians." (W. Reeves.)
(viii) Surette and Mason ... ... "The Appreciation of Music." (Novello.)
(ix) Edward Dickinson ... ... "The Art of Listening to and Appreciating Good Music." (Wm. Reeves.)
(x) Sir C. Villiers Stanford ... "Musical Composition." (Stainer & Bell.)
(xi) Sir Hubert Parry ... ... "Style in Musical Art." (Macmillan.)
(xii) H. Plunket Greene ... ... "Interpretation in Song." (Macmillan.)
(xiii) René Lenormand ... ... "A Study of 20th century Harmony." (Vol. 1.) Harmony in France to 1914. (Joseph Williams.)
(xiv) Mosco Carner ... ... Ditto. (Vol. 2.) "Contemporary Harmony." (Joseph Williams.)

APPENDIX III.

CHRONOLOGICAL TABLE OF THE MOST FAMOUS COMPOSERS.

This table does not profess to be exhaustive, and it does not include the names of writers anterior to the period at which modern instrumental music may be said to have had its birth, viz., the later years of the 17th century.

The nationality of each composer is indicated by a capital letter in brackets, thus: (A).= Austrian; (B).= Belgian; (Bh).= Bohemian; (Br).= British; (D).= Danish; (F).= Finnish; (Fr).= French; (G).= German; (H).= Hungarian; (I).= Italian; (N).= Norwegian; (P).= Polish; (R).= Russian.

Jean Baptiste Lulli (I).
(1633–1687)

Henry Purcell (Br).
(1658–1695)

Arcangelo Corelli (I).
(1653–1713.)

Alessandro Scarlatti (I).
(1659–1725.)

François Couperin (Fr).
(1668–1733.)

Johann Sebastian Bach (G).
(1685–1750.)

George Frederick Handel (G).
(1685–1759.)

Domenico Scarlatti (I).
(1685–1757.)

Giovanni Battista Pergolesi (I).
(1710–1736.)

Giuseppi Tartini (I).
(1692–1770.)

Carl Philip Emanuel Bach (G).
(1714–1788.)

Johann Christian Bach (G).
(1735–1782.)

Christoph Willibald Gluck (G).
(1714–1787.)

Joseph Haydn (A).
(1732-1809.)

Wolfgang Amadeus Mozart (A).
(1756–1791.)

Luigi Boccherini (I).
(1743–1805.)

Daniel Steibelt (G).
(1765–1823.)

André Erneste Grétry (B).
(1741–1813.)

Maria Luigi Cherubini (I).
(1760–1842.)

Johann Ludwig Dussek (Bh).
(1761–1812.)

Ludwig van Beethoven (G).
(1770–1827.)

Franz Schubert (A).
(1797–1828.)

François Auber (Fr).
(1782–1871.)

Ludwig Spohr (G).
(1784–1859.)

CARL MARIA VON WEBER (G).
(1786–1826.)

Johann Nepomuk Hummel (G).
(1778–1837.)

Gioacchino Rossini (I).
(1792–1868.)

Giacomo Meyerbeer (G).
(1791–1864.)

Gaetano Donizetti (I).
(1797–1848.)

Vincenzo Bellini (I).
(1801–1835.)

FELIX MENDELSSOHN-BARTHOLDY (G).
(1809–1847.)

ROBERT SCHUMANN (G).
(1810–1856.)

FRANÇOIS FRÉDÉRIC CHOPIN (P).
(1810–1849.)

Hector Berlioz (Fr).
(1803–1869.)

William Sterndale Bennett (Br).
(1816–1875.)

Niels Gade (D.)
(1817–1890.)

RICHARD WAGNER (G).
(1813–1883.)

Franz Liszt (H).
(1811–1886.)

Giuseppi Verdi (I).
(1813–1901.)

César Franck (B).
(1822–1890.)

Charles François Gounod (Fr).
(1818–1893.)

Friedrich Smetana (Bh).
(1824–1884.)

Joachim Raff (G).
(1822–1882.)

Anton Rubinstein (R).
(1829–1894.)

JOHANNES BRAHMS (G).
(1833–1897.)

Charles Camille Saint-Saëns (Fr).
(1835–1921.)

Max Bruch (G).
(1838–1920.)

Georges Bizet (Fr).
(1838–1875.)

Peter Ilitsch Tschaïkowski (R).
(1840–1893.)

Antonin Dvořák (Bh).
(1841–1904.)

Jules Massenet (Fr).
(1842–1912.)

Edvard Grieg (N).
(1843–1907.)

Arthur Sullivan (Br).
(1842–1900.)

Alexander Campbell Mackenzie (Br).
(1847–1935.)

C. Hubert H. Parry (Br).
(1848–1918.)

Charles Villiers Stanford (Br).
(1852–1924.)

Edward Elgar (Br.)
(1857–1934.)

Richard Strauss (G).
(1864– .)

Frederick Delius (Br).
(1862–1934.)

Claude Debussy (Fr).
(1862–1918.)

Alexandre Glazounow (R).
(1865–1936.)

Jan Sibelius (F).
(1865– .)

Alexander Scriabin (R).
(1872–1915.)

Ralph Vaughan Williams (Br).
(1872– .)

Gustav Holst (Br).
(1874–1934.)

Maurice Ravel (Fr).
(1875–1937.)

Igor Stravinsky (R.)
(1882– .)

Arnold Bax (Br.)
(1883– .)

APPENDIX IV.

GLOSSARY OF TERMS.

THIS Glossary has been compiled as a help both to the reader of this volume—during the course of which certain of the words here included have been used—and also to the musical amateur who may meet with certain terms and expressions in programme-books and musical criticisms, concerning the meaning of which he may be in doubt. Within the limited space possible, the Glossary cannot hope to be thoroughly complete; but it is hoped that it is comprehensive enough to be useful.

Allemande.—A dance of German origin occurring in the Suites of the older composers.

Bagatelle.—A short sketch (*e.g.*, the "Bagatelles" of Beethoven).
Ballad.—A simple song, in which the different stanzas are sung to the same music.
Ballade.—(i) A descriptive musical setting of a poem (*e.g.*, the "Walpurgisnacht" of Mendelssohn); (ii) a name given by Chopin and others to certain pianoforte compositions of variable form.
Barcarolle.—A composition based on the idea of a Venetian Gondola song, generally in $\frac{6}{8}$ or $\frac{12}{8}$ time.
Binary.—A term used to indicate the form of a movement consisting of two main divisions, or parts.

Cadence.—The completion of a phrase, or musical period, giving the idea of musical "punctuation." (*See* pages 15–19.)
Canon.—Strict imitation by two or more voices or parts.
Cantata.—Formerly a vocal solo of dramatic character; nowadays a work for chorus and orchestra, with or without solo voices.
Canzona.—A name formerly given to certain pieces written in more or less strict imitation.
Canzonet.—A short song (*e.g.*, Haydn's "My mother bids me bind my hair").
Capriccio. / *Caprice.*—An instrumental solo, somewhat irregular in form.
Carol.—A song of joy or devotion, usually associated with Christmastide.
Chant.—A short composition, adapted for the musical recitation of the Psalms, &c.
Choral, or Chorale.—A German Hymn-tune.
Chorus.—(i) A composition sung by a body of voices, several to each part; (ii) The refrain or burden of a song.
Chromatic.—Notes contrary to the key-signature, but not causing a change of *key*.
Clavichord.—A keyboard instrument, one of the precursors of the Pianoforte.
Coda (lit. a "tail-piece").—A passage of greater or less interest intended to emphasize, or to heighten the effect of, the conclusion of a composition. (*See* page 40.)

Concerto.—A work for a solo-instrument, with orchestral accompaniment, very much on the plan of a Sonata. (*See* page 55.)
Counterpoint.—A melody added to, and running alongside of, another melody.
Courante.—One of the dance-movements in the old Suites.
Czardas.—A Hungarian national dance.

Development.—The name given to the second division, or *part*, of a movement in Sonata-form. (*See* page 43.)
Diatonic.—Notes indicated in, or implied by, the key-signature of any particular key.
Dominant.—The name given to the 5th degree of the scale.
Double-Counterpoint.—A Counterpoint (*q.v.*), which sounds equally well above or below a given melody. (*See* page 47.)

Episode.—A theme of secondary importance, occurring once during the course of a movement.
Exposition.—The name given to the first main division, or *part*, of a movement in Sonata-form. (*See* page 43.)

Fantasia.—A composition somewhat in the style of an improvisation.
Fugue.—A contrapuntal composition, developed from a short theme, called its Subject.
Full Score.—The parts for an orchestra (with or without voices), ranged one above another on the same page, on different staves.

Gavotte.—A moderately quick dance, in $\frac{4}{4}$ time, beginning at the half-bar.
Gigue.—One of the dance-movements in the old Suites; it is quick and lively in character, and usually in $\frac{6}{8}$ or $\frac{12}{8}$ time.
*Glee.**—A piece of unaccompanied vocal music in at least three parts, for solo voices, usually those of men.

Harmony.—Sounds in combination.
Harpsichord.—A keyboard instrument, one of the precursors of the Pianoforte. Its strings, instead of being struck by hammers. were plucked by "jacks," or quills.

Impromptu.—An instrumental composition having somewhat of the character of an improvisation. (This term has been used notably by Schubert and Chopin, as the title of certain pianoforte pieces.)
Intermezzo.—A short movement connecting other larger divisions of a sonata, symphony, etc. The term was also used to describe short instrumental pieces in the early Operas.
Inventions.—A term used by J. S. Bach for two sets of small pianoforte pieces (15 in two parts and 15 in three parts), each developing a single idea.

Key.—A series of sounds, in relation to one particular sound called a *key-note.*

Leading-note.—The name given to the 7th degree of the scale.
Lessons.—An old English term used to designate sets of dances similar to those in the *Suite.*
Lied (German).—A song.
Lieder ohne Worte.—Songs without words. A term given by Mendelssohn to 48 short pianoforte pieces of a lyrical character.

---

* *See* foot-note to *Part-song.*

*Madrigal.**—A short contrapuntal choral composition for three, four or more voices, unaccompanied; largely cultivated during the 16th and early 17th centuries.

Mass.—A choral setting, with or without accompaniment, of certain portions of the Eucharistic Service in the Roman Church. Sung in Latin.

Mediant.—The name given to the 3rd degree of the scale.

Minuet.—Originally a slow and stately dance in $\frac{3}{4}$ time. Quickened by Haydn and Mozart.

Modulation.—Change of key.

Moto perpetuo.—An instrumental movement, in which a ceaseless flow of rapid notes is maintained throughout. (*See* Finale of Weber's Pianoforte Sonata in C major, No. 1).

Movement.—A self-contained section of a musical work, separated from the rest by a change of time or of key, or both.

Nocturne. / *Notturno.*—Originally a serenade; now an instrumental piece of a somewhat gentle and tranquil character.

Opera.—A musical drama. In *Grand Opera* the whole work is set to music; in the French *Opéra Comique*, and the German *Singspiel*, the musical portions are interspersed with spoken dialogue. This is also the case in English light opera.

Opus (generally abbreviated thus:—*Op.*)—Lit., a work. A term used to denote the *number* of a composition of any particular composer, in order of publication.

Oratorio.—An extended composition for solo voices, chorus and orchestra, usually illustrating some sacred subject.

Overture.—(i) A Prelude to an opera or an oratorio; (ii) A concert-piece for the orchestra, usually in Sonata-form

*Part-song.**—A short choral composition, usually of a simple, melodious character.

Pedal.—A note (generally in the bass) sustained through a succession of changing chords.

Phrase.—A musical period (frequently of four bars).

Recapitulation.—The name given to the third main division, or *part*, of a movement in Sonata-form. (*See* page 43.)

Recitative.—Musical declamation, the rhythmic shape of which is entirely governed by the words to which it is set.

Related keys.—Keys having the greatest number of notes or chords in common.

Requiem.—A Mass for the dead.

Rhapsody.—A composition of irregular form, in the character of an improvisation. (*See* the Rhapsodies of Liszt.) The fine Rhapsodies of Brahms for the pianoforte are, however, compositions of a particularly clear and coherent structure.

Rhythm.—The division of music into intelligible periods. (Often used also as signifying Lilt, Metre and Accentuation.)

Ritornello.—A short interlude, played before or after, or between the parts of, a song.

Romance. / *Romanza.*—A term often applied to a short instrumental piece of romantic character.

---

* The expressions Glee, Madrigal, and Part-song, should be carefully distinguished from one another.

Sarabande.—One of the dance-movements of the old Suites; of slow and dignified character, in $\frac{3}{2}$ or $\frac{3}{4}$ time.
Scena.—A dramatic solo for the voice, usually with orchestral accompaniment.
Scherzo.—A composition of a playful, humorous character. The successor of the Minuet as the third movement in most modern Sonatas and Symphonies.
Sentence.—A musical period, consisting of two or more phrases.
Sonata.—An instrumental composition, of at least two movements, *one* at least of which must be in what is technically known as Sonata-form. (*See* pages 54–55.)
Spinet.—One of the precursors of the Pianoforte. Like the Harpsichord, its strings were plucked with "jacks" or quills.
Study.—A composition for the overcoming of some special technical difficulty.
Subdominant.—The name given to the 4th degree of the scale.
Submediant.—The name given to the 6th degree of the scale.
Suite.—A series of short instrumental pieces, often in dance-form. The old classical Suites, of which those of Bach and Handel are the finest specimens, usually contained the following dances, *viz.*: Allemande, Courante, Sarabande and Gigue, to which others were sometimes added.
Supertonic.—The name given to the 2nd degree of the scale.
Symphony.—An orchestral composition of the form and character of a Sonata. (*See* pages 54–55, and also Chapter XI.)

Ternary.—A term used to indicate the form of a movement consisting of three main divisions or parts, the third of which is more or less a repetition of the first.
Thematic Development.—The working-out of a theme, by means of which that theme assumes certain changes of character and feeling. (*See* pages 8–10.)
Toccata.—An instrumental composition intended to shew off the touch and execution of the performer. (Bach uses the term on several occasions; *see* his Toccata and Fugue in D minor for the organ.)
Tonic.—The name given to the first degree, or key-note, of a scale.
Trio.—A term used to denote the second or alternative Minuet, Gavotte, etc., played after a principal one. So called from the fact that the earliest specimens were written in three-part harmony. (*See* page 44.)
Tutti.—All. A term used, principally in orchestral music, to denote that the whole body of performers is to play. Usually met with during the course of a Concerto.

Unison.—The same sound produced by two or more voices or instruments. N.B.—Male and female voices, when they sing in octaves, are described (inaccurately) as singing in *unison*.

Viol.—The precursor of the modern Violin.
Virginals.—A keyboard instrument, a precursor of the Pianoforte. It is said to have received its name as a compliment to Queen Elizabeth, the "Virgin" Queen; this view of the origin of the name is, however, very doubtful.
Vocal Score.—Vocal parts ranged one above another on the same page.
Voluntary.—An organ solo, played before, during, or after, any portion of the Church Service.

GENERAL INDEX.

*** Terms, etc., found under their respective headings in the Appendices on pages 149-162 are not included in this Index, unless they are also mentioned in preceding chapters. The initials (f.n.) after the number of a page indicate that the particular subject specified is referred to in a *foot-note* on that page.